creating a leader

simply YOU

STAGE THREE

creating a leader

Kelly A. McCormack

Carbondale, Illinois

Creating a Leader LLC
Publishing Division
1740 Innovation Drive
Carbondale, IL 62903
www.creatingaleader.com

Printed in the United States of America
First Printing, 2019
ISBN 978-1-945943-02-7

Edited by Leslie Conner and Nick Gugliotti.
Cover and interior design by Desktop Miracles.
Interior formatting by Kelly McCormack.
Illustrations by Kelly McCormack.

welcome back

STAGE TWO was a deep dive into increasing your power by understanding your comfort zone. STAGE THREE is where you get to have fun and use your newly found power.

This part of the journey starts with *envisioning* what you want to create in the world around you. Then, we look at how to *execute* that vision in flow or in "the zone." Third, we will work to envision and execute in a way that *empowers* others who are influenced by what we create. And, finally, we look at how to continuously *develop* ourselves to increase our leadership score – the power we have to create

STAGE THREE incorporates all the learning from STAGES ONE and TWO. We will do this in a functional way – as you create what you would like to see in the world. We will clarify visions, select goals, take action steps, and overcome obstacles. Some of these obstacles are the same ones we looked at in the first two books. We find great incentive to overcome limiting programming – in pursuit of meaningful visions and goals.

In the first two books, you became competent in the comfort zone of your human complex and filled any major cracks. This book helps you grow your comfort zone – rapidly! That translates into even more power and ability to create.

Enjoy the adventure!

contents

Welcome back, Leaders! This final book in the series will be a journey through the tools and frameworks of creating as a leader.

Now that we have seen some of the challenges with our power to create, let's look at how we can bring more of our own visions into reality. This will help us to continue our "internal" work as we enjoy better results in the "external" world. Have fun!

CHAPTER ONE

visioning

Leaders create by executing visions.

We must raise our expectations of ourselves if we are to improve the conditions of our lives, the lives of those around us, and the health of society – locally and globally.

Our standards have been passed on, generation to generation. The quality of those standards has been slowly hijacked. Advertisements are designed to manufacture a false need, producing a daily fight-or-flight response. We have a myriad of unhandled symptoms that come from a technologically connected – interpersonally (somewhat) disconnected way of living. It has been quite a journey to go from 1.7 billion humans on the planet in 1919 to 7.7 billion today – and growing!

We need to be our healthiest selves, fully empowered, and able to create skillfully. Let's see how we can accomplish that.

The Leadership Score™ contains the new definition of leadership:

The Power to Create

Within this framework is a scale that allows us to measure the quality and quantity of *our own* power to create. The scale ranges from a worth-damaging state of comparing, -10, to a fully integrated and skillful state of creating, +10. The first and second books focused on some of the "invisible" aspects of our human complex that move us up and down that scale.

the leadership score

	power to CREATE	visioning	executing	empowering	developing
+10	**creating**	all possibilities visible	effortless	inspiring	continuous
0	**neutral**	neutral	neutral	neutral	neutral
-10	**comparing**	all obstacles visible	limited	discouraging	non-existent

We will now explore the actions of a leader. Creating is implemented through *visioning, executing, empowering,* and *developing.* Within each of these 4 components we find a range that spans from -10 to +10. Each gives us a new portal to improve aspects of these abilities that are critical for us to create. They work to highlight specific deficits in our human complex.

This is Part Two of the operating instructions started in the second book. We are exploring the features of the human complex. Let's take the adventure through each action – and the frameworks that make them more accessible – starting with visioning.

Visions can change our world.

Visions can also change our internal world.

When a leader learns to use visioning well – as the first step of creating – the seed of something new can be sown. Without a fully formed vision, the seed dies and has no opportunity to become a new business, home, skill, relationship, or way of life.

Part of our communication includes talking about our dreams. A small percentage of us take our dreams to the next step of realization. This step is called visioning. There are many excuses for us to hold onto dreams that are never materialized, many of which are subconscious.

Most of us have never been taught the *skill* of visioning as a practical tool for success and satisfaction in life. We can't create without the use of the components of the formula to create. Fortunately, the basics of these components are relatively easy to learn and use, especially after we have been working on improving our human complex.

Let's look at the difference between skillful and unskillful visioning. This will help us step into the process of visioning.

possibilities or obstacles

While I am writing this book, I will be stopped incessantly and have little flow in my communication if I engage my internal editor. Rule #1: When I am writing, I am NOT editing. This rule goes across the board in every creative endeavor. If we create and edit at the same time, we engage two opposing networks in our brain. In other words, we can't do both well. We will get some hybrid network in our brain that is not quite creating and not quite editing. By doing this, we have already lowered our Leadership Score before we ever start.

We are committed to the process while we are visioning.
We are committed to the process while we are editing.

A person who is unskilled at visioning uses this editing function prematurely. Such a "leader" can only see the *obstacles* that get in the way of creating a desired vision – editing the vision before it is complete. If you have ever had the "pleasure" of visioning with someone in this state, it is a test of relationship skills and patience…at best.

The flow of creativity is stopped at every turn because that person is not open to the complete creative process. They want to "manage" the creative process while it is still being flushed out. This is not an ideal way to operate.

The leader who sees all *possibilities* is on the opposite end of the spectrum from the obstacle-laden, -10 leader when it comes to visioning. There is a specific method to seeing this way – to not killing the seed before it can be sown. The -10 leader smashes, burns, and pulverizes the seed with a seemingly harmless misuse of editing. This is often disguised as "being realistic." They feel the need to self-protect.

Failed past endeavors might make the obstacle-laden leader feel the need to stop the +10 leader. None of us are wrong in this, only unskilled in the creating process. We can change that.

futureCam

To become competent at the process of visioning as a +10 leader, let's use the tool called the futureCam. This tool is a combination of time machine and sensory suit that provides an easy method to engage in a *possibility mindset.*

This is a sculpting tool for our future.

futureCam is a full-body experience that takes advantage of the recording function we have in our nervous system. Visioning requires a depth of full-sensory imagination, facilitated through the skillful use of attention. Focusing attention is a method of energizing the object of a vision with positive feelings. Let's put all this together in an exercise.

Honey, how does your future look in there?
futureCam
Year: 2024
Oh, it's really great! AND getting better by the minute!

Do this when you can create a relaxation state for yourself. The stress response will rob you of the *possibility mindset* necessary to do this exercise.

Imagine you have something you want to create (do, be, have, see, play, develop, share, etc.).

When you have a general idea of what that is, close your eyes. "Go to" a time when you would like to have that exist. It could be 5 months or 5 years from now, but pick a specific time.

Now that you are "in" this future environment, you have a special suit that allows you to control the 5 senses – sights, sounds, smells, tastes, and skin sensing – and your thoughts, feelings, emotions, inner sensations, and beliefs. It is like a full-body camcorder that picks up all sensory experiences – internally and externally.

You are in a 3-D, fully sensing environment. This is a recording, just like the recordings we have from our past. You can sculpt or paint every detail of this recording. Remember, no editing or statements like, "I can't do that." It isn't time for that. You can adjust the vision or the related goals later.

Make everything reflect the way you need and want it to be. By focusing your nervous system on what you don't want, you are left programming what you don't want. Not helpful! For example, picture specifics about your desired lifestyle, instead of obstacles or challenges. This positive campaign will help you avoid creating what you don't want while energizing what you do want – exponentially increasing your power.

Create the details of your vision. What are you wearing? Who is around you? What does the attainment of your vision look like, in detail?

What are the sounds, smells, tastes, and bodily sensations, inside and out?

What do you feel? What emotions are happening?

Remember, you are sculpting these. Make them what you want and need them to be. Choose the thoughts that support you while letting go of the ones that limit you.

What do you believe? What else do you believe about yourself, others, and the world? *Create* the experience of your senses deliberately, until it feels complete.

When your vision is created, "live" in it for a full minute. Feel it, think it, see it, and experience it fully.

You will likely want to do this exercise of stepping into the vision a couple of times a day. Do this for a minute in the morning as you wake up and at night just before sleep. These times take advantage of the slower brain waves that record this imagination exercise more rapidly in the nervous system.

Because this helps to make new connections in the brain's neurons (brain cells), I call this process Virtual Neural Reprogramming™, or VNR. The mind is not clear about what is real or what is imagined. This means the brain changes patterns and connections based on life's experiences AND what we imagine with full-sensory perception. Both of these give the nervous system its marching orders.

Therein lies "the law of attraction" for the object of your attention. You have engaged autopilot mode to do the work for you – to find the actions that will make whatever vision you hold, whether beneficial or not, come to fruition. That is why synchronicities seem to show up when one is skilled at the visioning process. A well-programmed autopilot function can make life that much more magical and fulfilling.

Hey, Sam, what are
you doing with that
fancy visioning tool
you've got there?

I am tweaking the
controls on my
Autopilot function
so it goes in the
direction I want it
to go. You can
borrow it when I am
finished if you want to.

Practice visioning. New skills become natural when we practice enough to become competent.

While practicing this skill, it is important to take visioning somewhat lightly. Often, leaders are afraid to take a firm position with a vision. Visions are more like a story being told right now that helps map a new future beyond your current comfort zone. The story can be adjusted as you go. Putting a stake in the ground allows you to observe the vision to see if it looks and feels right to you. If you practice stepping into your current vision frequently (VNR sessions), the revisions you make will be updated in the programming in your nervous system.

It is important to maintain *appreciation* for your current situation and environment *while* you hold the vision firmly in mind. This may seem like a small point, but it is not. If you concentrate on your current situation and it brings you into negative emotions, this will keep your power to create at a low level. Appreciation and gratitude can be immediate antidotes to negative emotions. Find much to be grateful for. Your future self will be grateful to you for it!

The sculptor appreciates the undefined clay as she holds her vision of what is to come and chips away at her masterpiece.

Life is a path. We get to evaluate, periodically, whether our current vision is still what we want – or not. We can adjust it based on new learning. This skillful use of intelligent mode – to change our autopilot programming – will better support us. We change our vision when it no longer serves us, or when another vision will serve us better. A new future-Cam session, along with VNR sessions (one-minute recall), will improve your vision and help you turn it into your reality.

troubleshooting

Challenge...

I can't hold my attention long enough to envision what I want.

Potential Steps...

Attention is so critical to the success of creating and implementing a vision. It is essential for so much of what we do in life. Having a diagnosed inattentive type of ADHD (reduced access to select where I place my attention), I get it! My brain isn't wired to be on my side to do these processes consistently or easily. Meanwhile, there are many things that can help to improve this.

Recognize that survival mode – the fight-or-flight response – will rob you of your vision-critical intelligent mode and possibility thinking.

Find a way to relax yourself...

Epsom salts baths, saunas, meditation, playing music, etc.
...and follow that with a visioning session.

Work more on troubleshooting areas covered in the second book. Find support when it is not moving along for you. This courageous step can help you eliminate unseen stressors that are unconsciously stealing your attention. Don't let them!

Credit yourself with any progress in the futureCam sessions. You are programming your new vision and beliefs. Any sign of improvement increases your *Power to Create.*

Challenge...

I can't stop editing while I am trying to do the visioning process.

Potential Steps...

Beliefs are the part of our autopilot system that limits the focus of our perception. ***A vision is already a type of belief – a limiter.*** For example, we wouldn't say, "I want to visit every square inch of the Universe. A vision would be more like, "I see my next vacation in Paris." When we edit while creating a vision, we further reduce its size and quality. Saying, "I would like to visit Paris, but I can't afford it," just killed that vision. Editing should come later, during the executing phase of creating. When we prematurely edit in the visioning exercise, we create a prison of beliefs that limit our capability. We become unfulfilled and have less access to flow mode. It is surprising what can be accomplished without these invisible shackles.

Ask yourself questions during the futureCam exercise.

What would I do if I couldn't fail?
If I had all the money that I needed to accomplish this?
If I hadn't experienced a heart break?
If I was supported in my efforts?

Ask any appropriate question to release the autopilot's limited programming that is working to reduce your vision.

Hold the vision as a possibility that you can act on or not.

This is something you are trying on for right now.
This is the story you are telling in this moment.

Learn all the steps of creating, so you don't edit at the visioning stage.

practical exercises

Exercise 1

Notice what you feel. This sounds like a silly statement, but most of us are so driven into stress mode we don't have time to see how we feel about what is going on around us and within us.

Exercise 2

When you get to a place where you know how you feel, find an area you would like to improve. This could be your next creation.

Exercise 3

Use the futureCam process to envision what you would like to create in your life as an improvement.

Exercise 4

Create a reminder to relive this new vision frequently using the VNR process.

Exercise 5

Work on the vision until it has become programmed in the autopilot system. You will recognize it as unconscious competence when the necessary skills have been committed to the nervous system, while actions are scheduled and acted upon daily. At this point, find the next area to be improved, developed, or expanded or the next adventure to be undertaken.

Exercise 6

Repeat…

I can see clearly now

The only thing Jennifer knew in this moment was that there was no way out of this situation. She had been mistreated to the point that she began to believe she deserved it. This was a lifetime low for her.

Unemployed, stressed, sick, and hopeless, Jennifer had reached a point of no return. Was it the loss of her business when she was younger? When her marriage fell apart? Was the illness in her body clouding her view of the world? These questions seemed to grip her in this pivotal moment.

Jennifer knew she had two choices: to give up or turn this around. She wanted so badly to quit because she saw no possibilities in front of her. But she decided she would move forward and give her life the best shot she possibly could.

At first, she couldn't muster the energy to find solutions. But she did envision that solutions would find her. They trickled in at first. She read about a battered woman who decided to live a different life. That woman healed and became a very successful entrepreneur and member of her new family.

She looked at many stories about people who had come from the bottom and picked themselves up. She still held great doubt, but she began to see a spark of hope.

That hope grew daily, as Jennifer took each step she saw in front of her. One day, she came across a new tool, the futureCam. As she engaged herself in the process, she noticed that all the doubt fell away, and she saw only possibility in front of her. This made her stand a little bit taller and shine a little bit brighter.

With such a drastic change in her state of mind, she

committed to the process. Within a few short weeks, Jennifer's health improved. Her energy increased dramatically. Every ounce of new energy she found was invested into clearing out the years of internal blocks and to building new visions.

A year later, Jennifer was ready to lead her company to its 5-year vision. She almost didn't recognize herself. Jennifer had a momentary flashback to the hopelessness of her past life. With a very humble and grateful smile she said, "Let's go make this world a better place."

In that moment, a visionary was born

Visioning is so much fun!
Imagine we get to tell a
story about what our life
will be like in a few months
or a few years. Most people
don't do this because they
kind of suck at the next
type of action -- *Executing*.
But the secret to success is
that executing our vision
in flow mode can be even
more fun than telling
the story about the future.
Buckle up!
We're going into "*the zone*."

CHAPTER TWO

executing

En"light"ening Leadership

Son, it doesn't look like you accomplished anything on this list I gave you yesterday!

Mr. Edison, I didn't think you were serious about that light bulb thingy you were talking about?!

While inspiration IS important,
master creator Thomas Edison reminds us
that perspiration is 99 times more important.

We know with certainty that the starving artist
hasn't executed every step that would lead him to success.

Once we understand the creation process…
successfully creating becomes a choice.

Nobody ever intends to watch their dreams die. "Middle-aged" has become synonymous with feelings of regret and is mired in the emotions of perceived failures of yesteryear. We are all doing our very best with the unconscious programming we have. We are all doing our best based on the skills we acquired that allow us to create the world around us.

Our best is dependent on our ability to envision clearly and meaningfully. If we learn to do that well, we can begin to work with that vision to skillfully execute it.

effortless or limited

Executing visions is an easy way to determine the current abilities of our human complex. Our +10-level of creating, or flow mode, is most recognizable in this stage. When we're clear about where we are going and have practiced the steps we need to take to a level of unconscious competence, there is a far greater chance we can create in an effortless way – *flow*.

When we are unclear about our outcome, missing competence in the action steps, and find ourselves mired in the stress response, we have a far more *limited* ability to execute meaningful visions. How many times have you tried to do something, but everything else got done *except* for that one task? Your human complex stands in the way or in support of your vision. If you have a poor attention span, low energy in body or mind, beliefs that continue to hold you back, or any other impediments to action, you will feel very limited in what you do.

If you have trained your attention, become energetic in body and mind, adjusted beliefs to support your goals and actions, and handled anything else that was in the way, you can find yourself in the seemingly effortless and time-bending state of flow mode.

The world is a very different place to live depending on the level from which you create. At -10 on the Leadership Score, I am very concerned with making sure others aren't getting more than I have. That way, I don't feel like I am falling behind due to my inability to create or execute a vision. At +10, I am not concerned with what others accomplish, unless I am able to co-create with them or support their efforts.

Oooh, SQUIRREL!

What the...!

???

Oh, Hi Mom!
I was just watching our dog's
attention span surpassing my
husband's. And, how are you?

Being in Flow

Have you ever seen someone in flow mode or been in flow yourself? It is magical, like a dance. We are moving with the object of our attention, and all else falls away. In that moment, we have no inner critical voice, only the feeling that what we are doing is bigger than ourselves. When we find this state, we are tapping into something that *is* bigger than our*selves*.

Every person who speaks of this state uses similar words. It doesn't seem to be *our* creative genius and magnificence in that moment, but it always feels terrific to be along for the ride.

This ultra-present state is +10 leadership. When we are in it, we have the programming in our human complex on our side. We produce all of the most potent, feel-good chemicals naturally. If we put ourselves in this state frequently, our bodies and minds can often heal themselves...miraculously.

Some also refer to the experience of flow as being in "the zone." Let's look at this further by bringing back *The Three Zones* model introduced in Book 2. Reviewing the model, we saw that staying in our comfort zone is a path to boredom. Going too far past our comfort zone can be overwhelming and can even reduce our comfort zone. But, there is a zone between the comfort and overwhelm zones that holds the ticket to fulfillment while executing our visions. This is the growth zone. It is so called because when we make skillful use of this middle zone, we can grow our comfort zone. Growth zone is an appropriate name for this area when we are focusing on improving and expanding our human complex. Another name for the growth zone when we are executing could also be, simply, "the zone."

the three zones

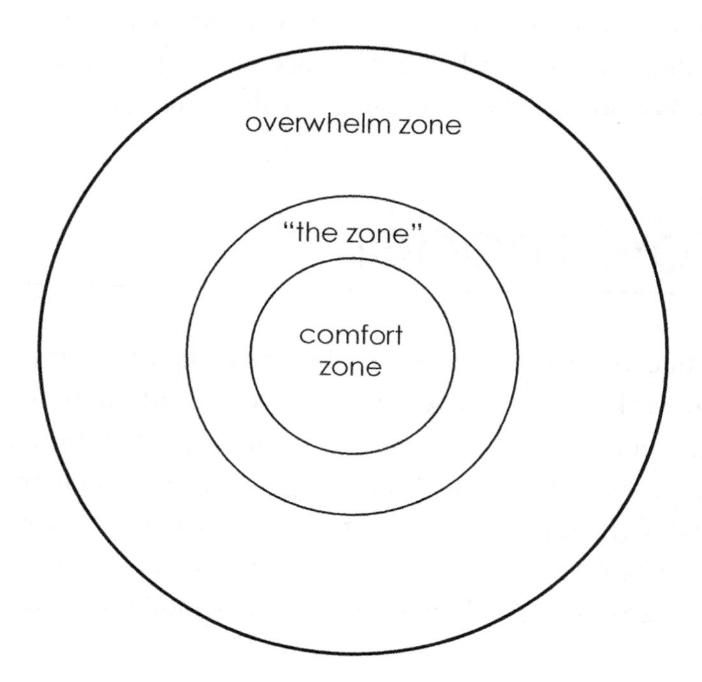

Further developing *the three zones* model into its relationship to executing our visions, we can refer back to the Leadership Score. We execute as leaders on a scale that goes from limited to effortless. There are three excellent indicators that tell us when we have reached flow or "the zone." I refer to them as the acronym SET. "S" is the *selfless* feeling of going beyond ourselves to something greater. "E" is for *effortless*, meaning we have practiced the execution of the skills that are needed to a point of unconscious competence. And, "T" is for the *timeless* feeling when time either stands still or passes rapidly.

When we reach this SET point, we have done our homework and are competent, we have gone beyond the programming in our comfort zone into a more creative place, and we are enjoyably seeing our meaningful vision become a reality.

I would be remiss to leave executing to chance based on this more theoretical three-zone model. That is why we have a framework that makes more of an art and a science out of finding "the zone" when executing a meaningful vision.

Let's look at that tool, called the *flow model*, now.

flow model

While we need to focus on our human complex – our "internal work" – to improve our ability to execute steps, we can incorporate that work into the creating process through a framework. The *Flow Model* helps to develop well-crafted goals to realize a vision. The more we experience flow mode, the more our human complex can repair its comfort zone and expand its capabilities. Finding flow mode is the key.

This framework is rooted in millennia-old and brand-new structures that I have developed and brought together. It allows us to use intelligent mode to create from where we are right now. We can then expand as we improve our comfort zone with adequate competencies, supportive beliefs, and a healthy, relaxed nervous system.

We engineer flow as part of a creation cycle.

Let's look at the *flow model* in steps. First, the basic structure includes a space for some details of the *vision* that we created in the futureCam process. We take that vision and break it into a *goal* or *goals* that will be a stretch, yet manageable for where we are. Each goal is accomplished by identifying *actions* to be taken and executing them. Additionally, the *obstacles* that must be overcome are identified and turned into action steps, then removed from this category.

When we work skillfully to balance each of the components on the triangle while aiming to find "the zone," we will experience more flow.

Vision

We always start with a vision because that is the destination we programmed in the futureCam session. It represents our desired outcome. Describe that experience, at the top of the *flow model*, in a few words that will help you fully associate with your full-sensory futureCam vision.

Flow Model

Basic Triangle

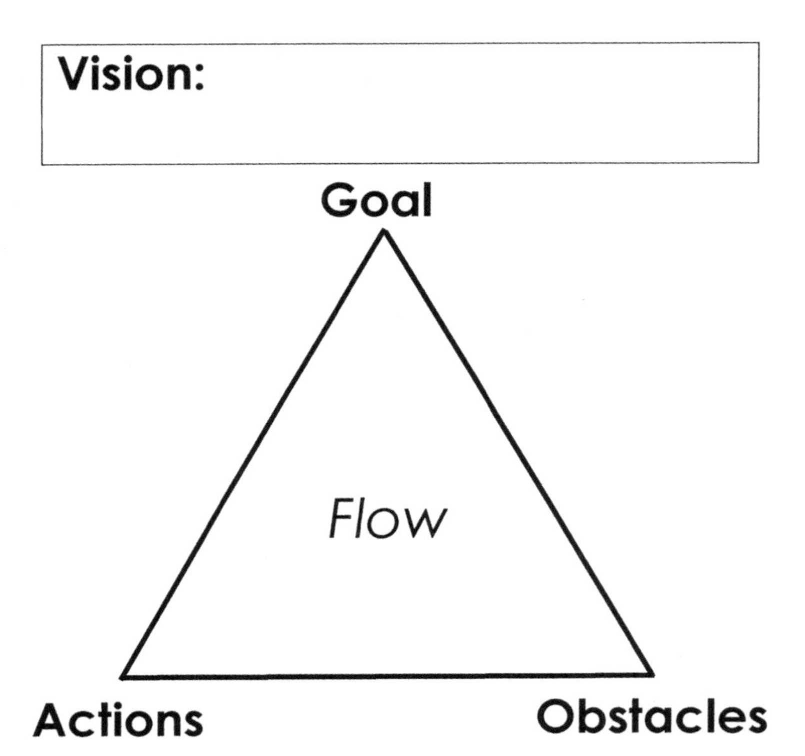

It can be helpful to do a draft of a story board with the vision as it is. I call it a story board, instead of a vision board, because it can seem easier to change the story's details as more information becomes available. Use pictures, words, art, poetry, or anything that associates you with your senses from the futureCam session. This supports you in clarifying your new vision and committing it to autopilot. The more playful and supportive you are with this part of the process, the greater chance to succeed in creating. With your vision in mind, let's create a triangle – starting with the *goal*.

Goal

Engage the *possibility mindset* while you select a portion of the vision you could reduce to a first goal. If you saw yourself in an improved relationship with a career you are passionate about and a very healthy, energetic body, pick one of those to use as your first goal toward realizing your ultimate vision. Write down the goal. Include a date and meaningful quantities/qualities that would stretch you if you achieved them.

Action

Action is a component of executing that is part tangible, part "magic." The tangible part is any known step that can be taken right now. The "magic" part occurs when we take the steps that are clear to us and suddenly new steps appear – seemingly out of nowhere.

For example, Elon Musk is creating affordable solar power for homes, electric cars, and reusable rockets. These are written here as loosely clarified goals that came from his vision. We need to take one of those and clarify it further – *reuse the Stage 1 portion of a rocket by 2017.*

If Elon has a rocket in place and wants to reuse the part that makes it capable of taking off, engineering is needed. That is the first action that would come under this vision. Once the engineering is complete, they would build and test this new rocket to see if they can reuse the Stage 1 portion. As of March 2017 when his team accomplished this feat – the first of its kind – Elon had envisioned creating something very specific and took ALL of the actions to realize that goal.

Most of us are not engaged in rocket science in our own lives. But we use the same steps to create and execute our own meaningful vision and goals. Identify and take the actions that are clear – others will "show up."

We must show that we are serious enough to take the steps in front of us. That helps to reveal the next possible steps. We can associate this to our courage and responsibility dials and other parts of our autopilot and intelligent modes. Identifying the actions that can be taken – and taking them – is an important part of creating successfully.

Increasing our *resourcefulness skills* will support our abilities to create in this step of the process. I like to practice this as a game by asking myself, "What are 10 ways I can take care of this issue?" Then, I can select one or two viable options.

Actions to attain a goal require a *gap analysis*. We must know, with great clarity, where we are. Emotionally, we appreciate the current state, while being very honest about the reality of the situation. We also become very clear about the details of the goal. "World peace" will never do anything. Nor will "build a business," "get a relationship," or "become healthy." Here is where honesty and knowledge will generate *potential* Power (to Create).

If your goal is to have a business that serves high-energy, healthy food to 200 people per day, you probably could write out 100 steps to get started on that goal. This clarity helps illuminate the gap that exists between the current situation and the goal. I can clearly see the specific challenges I am resolving and the actions that would help me do that. Using resourcefulness, I will close the gap.

Obstacles

Life could be viewed as a process of overcoming obstacles in a manner that makes us stronger. It may be easier to decide what obstacles we are ready to face, and to face them on our terms when possible.

Obstacles can include anything that stands in the way of realizing our vision or goals. These could include deficits in our competencies, limiting beliefs, non-resilience of the nervous system, inflexibility in our control panel, financial deficits, lack of energy, negative relationships, lack of time, and unclear visions and action steps.

If obstacles are the "enemy" to our fulfillment, then we must name them to know what they are. Often the battle is won just in the naming of the obstacle. It is no longer a "fight."

These obstacles are great tools for us to learn and grow. We can name an obstacle, use the gap analysis to see where we are and where we want to be, and then employ the resourcefulness tool. We can move the obstacles over to actions and simply take the steps necessary to overcome them.

As we shall see, without obstacles, we will usually struggle to find our own flow mode. Obstacles can sculpt us, but we will want to choose the right amount to overcome.

You're clearing hurdles
without any problem now!
Clear Action
Knowledge
Yes! Obstacles
seem to disappear
almost as soon as I
know what they are.

The Interaction of Goals, Actions, and Obstacles

Have you ever noticed that when you are given a task that does not challenge your abilities, you might not feel engaged in the activity? You might be bored or feel like you are not fulfilling your potential.

On the other side of the coin, have you ever taken on more than you could possibly be comfortable doing? It might initiate the stress response in your nervous system. With that, the capacity to engage intelligent mode is reduced or extinguished.

There is an optimal amount of challenge for each of us. It helps us fulfill our potential, while we realize our vision. When managed, challenge is also healthy and healing and can expand our capabilities at a very rapid rate. Flow mode is the indicator that we have accessed this optimal mix of goal, action, and obstacles.

How do we engage flow mode? How do we live in "the zone?" Do we really have control over the obstacles, actions, and goals? The short answer is "Yes." The *Flow Model* is designed for you to adjust any "lever" or point that would help you to achieve flow mode more reliably. That means that we can adjust any of the 3 areas of the triangle – increasing or decreasing the complexity – to find the right mix for our current capabilities, resilience, and resources. Any change in the complexity of one area, changes the other 2.

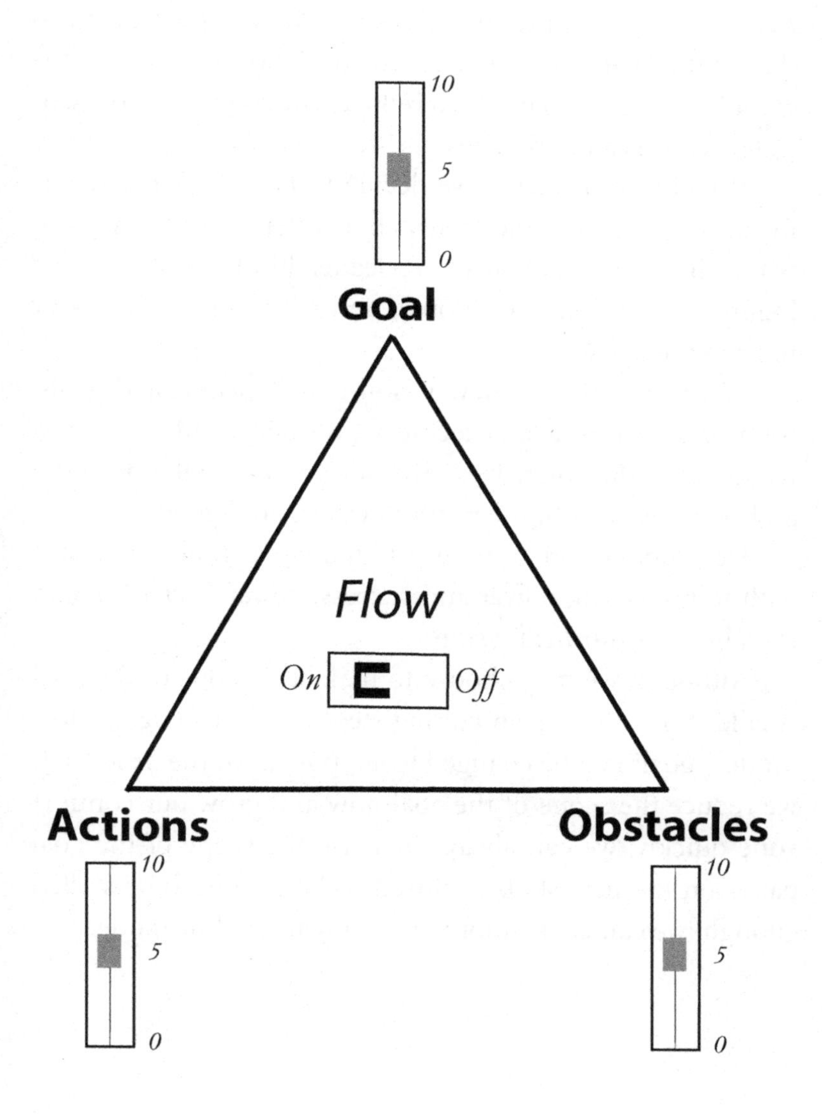
10
5
0
Goal
Flow
On
Off
Actions
10
5
0
Obstacles
10
5
0

If I create a very challenging goal, I can increase my skills and resources to overcome obstacles, or I can increase the actions that I take to attain the goal. I can also choose to reduce the complexity of the goal, which reduces the complexity of associated actions and obstacles

Whichever direction we decide to take, the objective is to turn on the flow mode switch as often as possible. That is the shortcut to our own +10-leadership level. It can be a highly productive, educational, and enjoyable path to our most authentic selves.

When we attain a new vision and its associated goals, we overcome obstacles, execute action steps, and create new resources within ourselves. This allows us to take on more and more responsibility in future visions and goals.

Developing and healing our human complex is a fast path to increasing power and success. *Power to create* could even become our next vision.

Although we may choose to make the scope of the goal smaller for now – as an editing step to help us engage flow mode – goals can be changed to support us in the process. If we reduce the scope of the goal now and grow our comfort zone quickly, we can always increase the scope of the goal based on the new skills acquired. When we become skilled enough, we can create more *while* staying in flow mode.

How is it going with "Creating a Leader?"

It's pretty dense! I thought I would take a break and watch a sunset while I let it all settle in.

The 3 "A's" of the Flow Model

We have seen how the scope of our goal affects our actions and obstacles. We can change any of these 3 areas to make our vision and flow mode more attainable.

There are 3 "As" that, when understood, further support operating in flow mode. These are *attachment, avoidance,* and *attention.* The first two are related to how we feel about the goal, actions, and obstacles with which we are engaged. If we are *attached* to the vision or the goal, we may experience the stress response with less access to our creative resources. Similarly, if we are trying to *avoid* obstacles or actions, we will likely find ourselves stressed and less capable of creating.

The secret weapon is the final "A," our *attention.* Skillful use of attention can supply energy to our goal, clarity to our action steps, and solutions to overcome obstacles. Our attention is like magic when we use it to focus into *this* very moment. Every second of life is like a frame in a film. The only way we can be stressed is if we compare one frame to another. Don't compare. Just make this frame the best you can with the time you have!

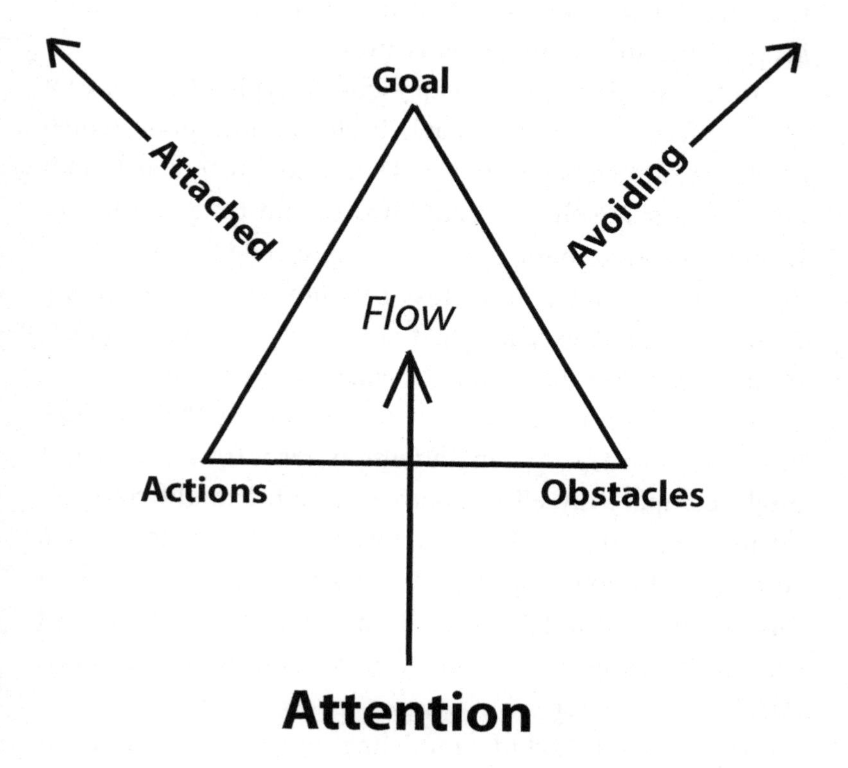
Goal
Attached
Avoiding
Flow
Actions
Obstacles
Attention

Flowing with Attention Skills

Imagine you have a frame in life, like the 24 to 30 individual frames that make up each second of your favorite YouTube video. If we call this moment in which we live a 1-minute frame, what would you do with this minute? If I am fully focused on this minute, I am only engaging in the words that I am typing. I know, with clarity, what my target is. I am keeping any and all distractions away.

In this single minute, I can focus on typing this concept of living frame-by-frame. That helps foster flow mode, which carries me timelessly until my 45-minute break alarm goes off. I am surfing the 1-minute waves, and time just passes without my awareness. I am only responsible for what I can do with this minute…now this one…now this one. Creating is about skillfully executing actions during each one-minute frame of our lives, based on our goals and our vision.

If I am comparing myself to something that is NOT in this moment, I take my attention away from creating. I might compare myself to another author. I might compare my missing skillset to the intense work that goes into writing, editing, and publishing three books. None of those exist in *this* minute. I would rob myself (and you) of this minute of creating by comparing myself or my work to another minute, standard, or person.

This doesn't exclude modeling others for actions or behaviors that would help to become more competent, when it makes sense for *our own* goals. Additionally, feedback is another important part of this process that can help us grow rapidly. When it is time to focus on these powerful resources, we do these actions during the current one-minute frame.

In the expanded diagram of the *Flow Model*, we see that attention is a fundamental skill for creating. When we compare current to past circumstances or to future challenges, we may feel like avoiding a perceived problem or attaching ourselves to specific outcomes and actions. We have taken a "frame" from our past, compared it with our goal or action step, and allowed it to hijack this minute from us. We become less focused on what we decided to do right here and right now. Our stress response is engaged, and we are no longer able to execute as well in support of our vision.

> We can direct our attention and get back into flow mode.

Notice when you experience a feeling of dread, stress, fear, or anticipation of a problem. Check in with yourself, handle any issues, and bring your focus back to the words you are typing, the grocery bag you are lifting, the 10 steps of the mile you are running, the conversation you are having, or the vision you are creating.

If you are avoiding (dreading) or attaching (craving), you have pulled in past and future frames to compare to the current frame. This robs you of the attention necessary for creating. You have to work to move past your limiting programming. To do that, you must see each moment as it is, not as you fear it might be. Only then can you move out of attaching to and avoiding past and future circumstances – *and back into flow.*

Creating and Balancing in Flow

When we become skilled with these tools, we can use them to quickly get into flow mode. We can create goals that bring our human complex into greater states. This keeps going around in a productive upward spiral. No matter where we find ourselves on the scale of the Leadership Score, these tools allow us to drop the impediments and move quickly into our most focused, productive, and fulfilling states.

We can learn to adjust goals so we can meet and handle appropriate obstacles. Executing steps to attain these appropriate goals will lead to greater fulfillment and more flow states.

We can achieve flow faster if we create a goal to bring our human complex to a new standard. We directly observe and eliminate obstacles that are programmed in the human complex. When we create this type of vision, we can get a major upgrade. If we don't see the obstacles or can't acknowledge them, we cannot upgrade. If there are self-esteem challenges which we are not willing to see and handle, we will be stuck with them. They will hold us back. *Honesty, courage, and responsibility are repaid through new abilities and power.* Practice makes honesty comfortable and easy.

The "payoff" is worth it!

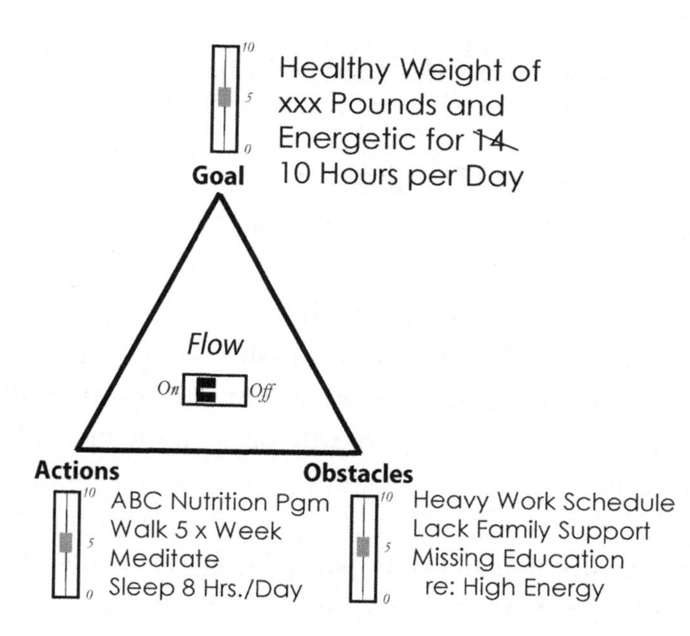

How is your
New Year's
Resolution
coming along?

Ever since I adjusted
the Goal to better match
the current obstacles,
I am moving along
effortlessly while everyone
seems to be more supportive.
I will probably raise the bar soon!

troubleshooting

Challenge...

I am not sure what step to take to attain my goal.

Potential Steps...

It is critical to know the details of what we want to create. We also want to clarify the mission and purpose of creating a vision and goals. Finally, we will focus on the first step to achieve our goal.

Clarify your vision and your detailed goal statements.

Use present language with your goals – as our autopilot tends to program what we say as a command. Past and future tense could keep you from having the object of your vision. Say "I'm grateful to have" instead of "I will have."

Capture the vision and goals on a story board.

Ask yourself "why" you are doing this. Get as many reasons as possible to upgrade the vision and goals from "nice to have" to a necessity. This is how we get our needs met. We don't necessarily do what we think is simply a "good idea." Ask, "Why?" to make this a necessity by clarifying the mission and purpose.

Take a step.

It doesn't have to be perfect or big. Small action steps taken consistently reveal other steps that lead to the goals and the ultimate vision.

Challenge...

I don't find it easy to identify obstacles.

Potential Steps...

The more we work on our human complex and create vision-attaining goals, the more visible the obstacles become. They are easily found when we decide we will create a certain goal. Within that goal, we begin to close the gap through actions – from where we are to where we need to be. When we find difficulty with executing those actions, we have identified an obstacle. It could be missing competencies, a limiting belief, a lack of resources – like time or money. It becomes a new goal to overcome that obstacle as a part of the bigger goal. If I am without the time necessary to write this series – a common occurrence – I create a vision to make the time. Now I can overcome that issue with clarity and power. From there, I am back to the book series.

Identify the goal with detailed clarity.

Act on what shows up in the gap.

Notice where it is challenging.

Create actions or goals to overcome the obstacles that challenge you.

Repeat to higher and higher skillfulness.

practical exercises

Exercise 1

Use a story board and daily VNR (one-minute vision reviewing) sessions to program the autopilot function with the vision.

Exercise 2

"Create" the minute you are experiencing right now – including the internal and external senses – to make this a productive and ideal minute. Do that several times until you experience intelligent mode.

Exercise 3

Set up time to work on the goal's action steps. Consciously use a minute-by-minute focused approach with your attention until this becomes programmed. With the step that you are executing, there is no past or future (comparisons) – only a vision and goal that is guiding the action of this step.

Exercise 4

Practice a gap analysis with a *small* obstacle.

Examples: Do one relaxation session for 10 minutes or find a competency deficit and spend 30 minutes learning.

Exercise 5

Practice resourcefulness by taking one obstacle and working out 10 solutions that would resolve the issue. Select the best option and implement it.

one moment at a time

Ted couldn't understand why his attempts to increase the size of his company were unsuccessful. He felt like he was in a rut. Ted had grown his company to 50 employees and had loyal and happy clients. He knew that his products and services were helping his clients and wanted to help more people through his business.

Ted decided that if he was going to increase his business, he would have to change his approach. He decided to take on the challenge of *creating a leader* within himself as his path to increasing his company's impact. As he discovered how his human complex could sabotage his success, he reflected on how little input he had been willing to accept from his staff. He knew immediately that he had beliefs from his childhood that were getting in the way. He was operating on the belief system that says, "They are trying to steal my ideas" and "I'll show them!" This kept Ted in a stress response that made him create more no matter what had already been created. He could see this pattern throughout his life now. He also saw how beliefs had blocked him from trusting his employees to do what they could for the company under his vision, goals, and policies. In fact, he realized he was running the company with a vague vision, at best.

Ted worked on changing his beliefs daily until he had replaced them with more empowering beliefs such as, "I create simply to share what I have to offer." With his new beliefs in place, Ted decided to do a futureCam session to create his company's vision. He "went to" 1 year in the future. There he saw himself relaxing, trusting others to do their work, co-creating solutions, and offering ideas for expansion.

He adjusted his beliefs in that moment to support the vision of a larger company that ran profitably and gave him balance in his life. There were 75 employees in this vision. His feelings would sometimes show up to block this view, but he adjusted those negative feelings in this future time and made a mental note to work on them after the futureCam session.

When he was satisfied with his clear and detailed vision of his staff, clients, and himself, he left the session. He documented his vision on a storyboard that would remind him of his experience of the 5 senses – including all visual representations, and his feelings, emotions, beliefs, and body sensations, as they existed in his vision. He understood that he had to keep the language of his new goals positive for his autopilot function to help make them a reality. He also kept his statements in the present tense, to further program his autopilot function correctly.

Ted could appreciate the current 50-person company he had built while concurrently holding a 75-person vision in mind. With such clarity of vision and gratitude for the current company, he did a gap analysis. He honestly assessed every part of the company as it stood in this moment. He then detailed the goals and compared them with the current situation. Now he knew some of the action steps and some of the obstacles that could be converted into action steps. He took his first step by pulling the team together and sharing his clarified vision. He expressed that he would be looking for more input as the team attained the goals. This brought up new concerns that Ted could explore in his human complex.

Ted was 4 months into attaining the new vision when he realized this projected 50% increase over one year could have a destabilizing effect. He adjusted the vision to a 30% increase. That put him and his team in flow mode far more frequently as they went through the year.

Ted and the team got the hang of the process. They could clarify the gaps that still existed, execute action steps, and watch the gap close more with each passing day.

The team was inspired when they could understand the goals and see how everything they did related to the greater vision.

Ted was amazed that handling his personal limitations had a direct effect on his ability to lead the company.

When they began to dedicate a section of the weekly meetings to address obstacles more fully, they found their progress was even more rapid and predictable. There was no longer a mystery around how they were attaining these new goals and realizing the vision.

With a string of action steps completed and obstacles overcome – having regularly found flow mode – they finished the year with a 40% increase and higher customer satisfaction and loyalty numbers.

They anticipated creating their next vision.

Ted was now ready to include his team in the visioning and goal-setting process, having handled his own obstacles to leading this process.

Ted's company became one of the most relaxed, yet engaged, places to work in the area. The employees were more likely to talk to each other about "hitting their stride" or overcoming an obstacle than last night's television show.

Ted knew he was engaged in a process that was benefitting his customers, his employees, his family, and himself. He smiled thinking back on the discomfort he avoided early in the process. It was now motivating him to learn more and expand.

Pretty straightforward:

With a clear vision in mind,
write the first goal statement.

Identify action steps
and take them -- when new
steps show up, take them.

Look for obstacles and
convert them to action steps.

Use your attention to create
the best you can in this minute...
now this one...and this one --
without comparing to anything.

Now I will share some of my story
to see how this whole process can
feel like quite an internal climb.
Enjoy!

the central story

"Inner Everest Expedition"

Mount Everest is 29,029 feet tall. That is cruising altitude for an airplane and twice the altitude of the perfectly good airplane I jumped from while attached to a guy wearing a parachute. The airplane makes the height seem less than it is. The lack of an airplane makes it very real!

It can feel that way in life. When we have the comfort of an established base camp, we don't have to experience the heights in life as scary or unprotected. Without that base camp, we can end up all over the mountain of life.

To climb Mount Everest requires something of a base camp. The one at around 17,600 feet is quite popular. This is the place where acclimation to the effects of altitude often begin. The average climber will spend the next 40 days climbing Everest in ways that will acclimate him, until he is ready to ascend one final time in hopes of reaching the peak.

In life, leaders are climbing their own inner Mount Everest. Some of us were given a great base camp by our parents or care givers. That means those parents were likely given a great base camp by their parents.

With such a base, the climb through life is a step-by-step approach to your potential that is marked by a comfort zone – established through your parents. Maybe your parents stayed down at the equivalent of base camp their entire lives. You learned to do the same. Perhaps they ascended to the peak – self-actualization, as Maslow called it – and you have followed in their footsteps.

These scenarios are dependent on the quality of your programming and the types of programming bugs that are present.

The best-case scenario would be that your parents were so healthy in their own lives, so skilled at parenting, that they helped you to establish a healthy path to fulfilling your potential in every area of life. But best-case likely doesn't exist. This person would be in a permanent type of autopilot mode if it did. It is more likely that the other scenario – parents staying at base camp or moving a little higher than that – happened.

But what happens when you didn't have an established base camp? What if you were given the best that your parents could offer yet their best fell short of what you needed to learn, to create supportive beliefs, and to establish a healthy nervous system? What if they didn't inherit what was needed for them to pass those skills down? This is all very common among those of us who remain frustrated in our attempts to create and realize meaningful visions.

Have you ever sat down to consider what this journey in life is really like?

If we are not prepared in life, if we don't have the right tools to set up base camp where it needs to be, we cannot live our lives at the peak of fulfilling our own potential. When that happens, the impact we can make in this world, along with the meaning life holds for us, can slip through our fingers.

Sometimes we feel this when a project isn't moving forward, we have challenges in our relationships, a vision or goal isn't realized, we experience financial distress, or a feeling inside says, "there must be something more."

It's possible to live and produce at a completely fulfilling level if we know how to navigate to that place. To do this, we may need a guide who is highly trained to navigate a mountain and help us climb to our peak of performance and creativity in life. At Mount Everest, that guide is known as a Sherpa. These guides have acclimated themselves to extremely high altitudes for generations. They have become experts at acclimating others to altitude and creating the safest path to peak experiences.

I had to become my own "Sherpa" in this process. I became very highly trained at navigating the steepest internal mountain. That came from immense experience at overcoming, what felt like, insurmountable obstacles and tragedies.

Imagine this as an inner journey. I have just arrived in Nepal. I have navigated the airports and days of hiking to find myself at base camp – 17,600 feet above sea level. I look up at the peak of my internal Mount Everest.

My tools for this trek will be the preparation that my parents had given me. We can hope that this autopilot function was programmed well enough to face the paths and challenges of life.

One way to understand the programming of this autopilot function is when you remember back to the first time you drove a car. You were responsible for the steering wheel, the brake, and the gas pedal. In addition, you had to put the car in gear and make sure that operating the vehicle wouldn't hurt anybody in your path. At that time, everything about driving was new to you, and you had to think about it consciously. At some point, after a lot of practice, your autopilot function took over. Now you can drive and read the paper, put on mascara, eat your breakfast, change the radio station, AND program your GPS. I have seen you – and let's hope your inner autopilot function IS carefully driving the car!

Our parents' role is to make our base camp – our autopilot function – as solid as it can be, so our trek in life will be as safe and successful as possible. But if they don't create a solid base camp because they didn't have one, what happens to us? What happens if your base camp isn't at 17,600 feet, the way others seem to be?

I didn't understand this inter-generational problem when I started out. I didn't know that at least 80 - 90% of us were not given a complete base camp that would support our journey to the peak in our lives, and that these deficits are passed from generation to generation. I had no idea that a ton of work had to be done just to reach a viable base camp.

My father was one of the very early program developers and systems analysts in our country. He was a very high-level genius – a brilliant man. He worked as a mainframe systems engineer and troubleshooter at IBM in the 60s and 70s and then at Bell Tel Labs – where they were developing the Unix operating system in the 70s and 80s.

Bell Labs was the Google or Apple of the 70s. The smartest and brightest minds from all over the world were there to create the future of technology.

One of the perks of having a dad who worked at Bell Labs was that I could play with a program, named ELIZA, that had been developed by the MIT Artificial Intelligence Lab in the mid-60s. Here I was, a young child in the mid-70s, talking to this computer who seemed very human-like to me, just like I had seen on Star Trek.

Although my father was a very talented technologist – excelling at his work – he had not received the internal programming necessary for complete well-being. He couldn't pass on what he didn't have.

He had created compensations for those areas in which his internal programming hadn't supported the fullness of his life. One of those compensations was alcohol, which would heavily contribute to his death – as it had with his mother.

That meant that I had received an autopilot function that was missing education and beliefs that would support the fulfillment of my own potential in life.

My mother can turn anything into beauty. Yet, she also inherited a base camp that would prove insufficient for stable footing during the climb of life. I inherited her instabilities, as well.

To start out climbing the mountain of life with faulty programs and a nervous system programmed in survival mode meant that I didn't have an established base camp. I kept falling further and further down the mountain.

At times, the falls would find me facing a great crevasse, like financial ruin. At other times, I would wait out a storm in my life – from which I couldn't be sure that I would ever emerge.

But there came a definite point when I said, "ENOUGH – I have to figure this out!" I couldn't just keep falling further down the mountain.

Starting that day, I would spend the next 3 1/2 years of my life climbing this mountain through some of the most treacherous conditions imaginable. I started down the path with a sinking feeling in my gut that maybe I shouldn't even attempt this climb. What if I don't survive this type of adventure?

I knew I was getting ready to face the possibility of storms that could keep me from getting to the peak of my life. The temperatures could plummet by the day as I approached the top and less support was available. I might find myself sick from the new altitude at any point in time. Because I didn't have eyes to see them, I could fall into a crevasse and even take the others who were tied to me down with me. Another avalanche of some sort could wipe me out.

The totality of the path that I was taking wasn't covered in the medical journals, the spiritual texts, or by the trusted scientists and philosophers from history to now.

When I am climbing to new heights and viewpoints, it can make others uncomfortable in the process. Our loved ones are not necessarily fond of change. Just as we have our own comfort zone, our *circle* enforces their comfort zone upon us.

And if all of that didn't keep me from the top, there was always the possibility of falling down the mountain – which is how my life had already felt to that point.

I was committed to summiting the internal Mount Everest of my life.

I had trained for this my entire life. But I would have to find and assemble the best possible team of mountaineers from all over the planet to get to the top. I would need new tools and technologies to help me see my own barriers and find ways to overcome and eliminate them.

First, I needed to know where I was. I wanted to make use of the best assessments I could get. I had my brain scanned twice at one of Daniel Amen's clinics. We found that I had the effects of ADHD present. That meant that the front part of my brain had too little blood flow for me to be able to function "normally" in my life. With a lifetime of concentration problems and reading challenges, it is no wonder I was dealing with some serious anxiety issues.

Additionally, a diamond-shaped pattern revealed in the scan showed the likelihood that I had been stuck in survival mode since childhood. I had had several traumatic experiences, according to the research of Kaiser-Permanente and CDC regarding Adverse Childhood Experiences – ACEs. Divorce and a family member attempting suicide are two of many experiences cited in the ACE study – both of which were a part of my history. This type of programming in childhood can devastate an adult, ripping away the comfort of a base camp that supports a lifetime of fulfillment and success. The negative effects on my life increased with time.

Current medical protocols had no solutions to my problems. With medicine or current therapies, I could only work on symptom management. But that wasn't going to be enough for me.

With other therapies, I could shut off a portion of survival mode in favor of the relaxation response. But I was stuck in a Hell that was getting worse – sometimes by the day. I wanted to live the life that I was meant to live, but I kept getting knocked down as these internal triggers seemed to fire off every minute of every day.

Nobody can live a fulfilling life if they are programmed to perpetually live in survival mode.

I needed answers immediately – while I still had the quality of attention that would allow me to find them. But what if my base camp was ripped apart? Could I still find my way to live at the peak of life? Could I still reach fulfillment?

With thousands upon thousands of hours of research and practice – using every resource of energy, time, attention, money, and networking available to me – I found the answers I was looking for. I found that the crevasses in my life were created by missing competencies, which amounted to my experiences and training. Remember the first time you sat in the driver's seat? The recorded experiences in your life and brain patterns didn't support you to be comfortable yet – you simply hadn't trained for that experience of life.

Because I was missing the competencies that would make me more capable of interacting with my life, I started making decisions about life that weren't accurate. These decisions are known as beliefs. They get programmed in our nervous system and further limit our ability to interact with life.

Imagine that my comfort zone is represented by a small circle, but my experience of life is much bigger – engulfing my comfort zone. Because my skillset and beliefs created an insufficient comfort zone to allow me to interact with my environment and life, I was overwhelmed by many circumstances.

That overwhelm – trauma – further programmed my nervous system to reduce my comfort zone when I encountered a circumstance that resembled any part of the recorded traumatic situations I had already experienced.

The crevasses were wide, and the bridges were unknown to me. During my climb, I experienced more episodes of falling down the mountain. Determined, I fortified myself with every possible solution that I could find. I turned over stones that I never dreamed would reveal aspects of myself that I needed to understand to go forward toward a solution – supplements, prescription drugs, spiritual practices, technological solutions for my brain and body, training sessions, and every related practice and practitioner license I could get my hands on.

Finally, I found answers that would take my constant

state of survival mode out of the hands of my limbic or emotional brain. That part of my brain had turned on the warning signal nearly 5 decades earlier and saw no reason to turn off the alarms.

But I learned the language of how we are programmed in our autopilot system. Then I learned how to reprogram it.

I learned what 3 areas get in the way of our ability to find ourselves in our most productive and creative state – known as flow – and found out how to build character muscles that would be critical if I was to succeed.

Flow is a state that enables us to be our most productive and creative and to enjoy life's circumstances. Flow feels like you are on top of the world. I hadn't experienced enough of this state because my survival mode was stuck in the "on" position – resulting in no control over attention and presence in my life.

I learned from Eastern practices and philosophies that I can actively manage attention well enough to find flow, but based on my condition, that could take decades of sitting on a meditation cushion.

I didn't have any more decades to give.

I learned from Western philosophy – Positive Psychology and their current tools for finding the state of flow – that attention can be sucked into an exhilarating activity if everything is present for that to occur. But the most consistent practitioners of this were riding 100-foot waves that made them look like ants?

That wasn't an option for me.

I needed a combination. I eliminated the programming bugs in my autopilot function that held me down from the state of flow. I adopted the Eastern practices to become present with the activity with which I was engaged. And I employed the Western use of engaging activities – only I would replace excitement with purpose-driven fulfillment of meaningful visions. Finally, I would need a very healthy body living on clean-energy foods.

With this recipe, I could live in a low- to mid-grade flow state for days, weeks, and even months.

I now knew how to work with these elements. I created a vision. I selected a well-crafted, stretch goal that took into account the state of my human complex and my current resources. I acted on the steps that I could see clearly. I identified the obstacles that held me back and overcame them.

If the obstacles were a past trauma or overwhelming situation that had become programmed, I could now handle that with my new-found tools: EFT and Matrix Reimprinting. I would release the freeze from my nervous system, find the limiting decision or belief that I had made in that moment, and support the resolution of the stuck video that was replaying. Now the effect of the freeze or bookmark in my limbic system, the belief, and the scene – all disturbing me below my conscious awareness – were released, one-by-one.

Using the *Flow Model* – vision, goal, actions, and the elimination of obstacles – each completed goal delivered new-found capabilities. Falling down the mountain or into a crevasse became an opportunity to find and explore the faulty programming that was present. I would reprogram according to the needs that I had for my current vision of life.

I now knew how to reprogram the subconscious mind

and improve my control panel that contained the character strengths that I possessed. I could use any activity to find this peak state of performance and creativity – known as flow. Finding the healing state of flow often, I was using that to produce a new, more stable state – a *stage* of living in flow. This was +10 leadership.

It worked. I arrived at the peak of my internal Mount Everest at 29,029 feet above sea level. *I could look out over the horizon from an entirely new vantage point.*

Three things happened to me whenever I would stand on top of that mountain. First, it was as if who I was fell away, and I was without a **self**. But because of the internal work I had done, it felt *amazing*. Next, everything I was doing became **effortless** – like I was riding a powerful wave. All of this while **time** stood still AND passed in the blink of an eye.

I created an acronym for this **S**elfless, **E**ffortless, and **T**imeless experience – SET. This is a SET point or entry point into flow. This point is where the Einsteins, da Vincis, Michael Phelps, and even the *father* who lays eyes on his child for the first time are born. This is the birthplace of genius, of flow, of being in "the zone," being in love, going beyond yourself, and creating at your highest level of potential.

The front part of my brain – where the inner critic lives, where my efforts are assessed, and time is experienced – went off line as something far greater emerged. I made use of my entire brain. And with my other wisdom, knowledge, practices, and tools, I could get to my SET point in record speed whenever I needed it to help me create something new.

For a moment, imagine in your mind's eye that you had started at base camp at 17,600 feet up on the mountain. You see the tents of the nervous fellow adventurers who will also ascend their internal mountain – against the odds and their comfort zones.

Now imagine moving through the crevasses, overcoming the weather conditions, surmounting the altitude, escaping slips that would cause you to fall down the mountain. You arrive at the top of your internal mountain – 29,029 feet above sea level and 5.5 miles into the sky. You look out for miles and see the peaks of the lower mountains. Your sense of self, effort, and time fall away as they are replaced with bliss and connection.

Living life from that place affords astounding increases in productivity, creativity, and learning. Leaders in that place understand the impact they will make with their visions. They will be so connected to themselves and everyone else that they will make decisions based on the highest positive and least negative impact. Their view is from their highest mountain and their connection is from their heart.

I found that being in flow would remove the "jackass" ways that can sometimes creep into our approach to vision and goal attainment, replacing it with "badass" productivity that makes the goals rapidly come to fruition. All of the badass without the jackass – what's not to like?

What could I do with this new ability to create at a far greater capacity, now that I was no longer spending my energy to keep faulty internal programming in place?

Perhaps I would use some of that to write a 3-book series to share the hard-fought learning and the discovery of tools that I used on my journey. Maybe I would become a "Sherpa" so that others could ascend their own internal mountains quickly and often, experiencing a new level of impact, fulfillment, and enjoyment in their lives. Maybe if I helped enough people to experience flow, they would help enough other people do the same. Flow increases our creative abilities to produce at a very high level while dropping the malignant, fulfillment-stealing comparisons that have ravaged our society's subconscious minds.

I don't know if it was all worth it when I fell down the mountain to sea level and below on so many occasions. But I will say that when I first stood on top of the mountain, **on top of the world**, I knew that my life was more stable than it had ever been. It seemed that a lot of good could come out of my journey, erasing the pain that had held me back.

So many of us who have an inadequate base camp could learn to fortify that base camp and stop a pandemic of poorly programmed autopilot functions. We are spending an inordinate amount of money to feel the feelings that are available to us in flow. It does require setting up base camp and leaving that comfort zone to explore and acclimate to new heights.

But, why do it? Why move out of the known and into the unknown? Why learn to create such a stable jumping off point? Why climb a mountain? Why engage flow? I asked these questions early on and got the answer when I arrived at the top of the mountain.

You fully deserve it
and
the world deserves
the fullness of you.

Moutaineering Kelly here.
It was quite a journey to recognize
the parts of the human complex
and the bugs that can make it
go off course. Even more fun
to see how clarifying visions and
executing well can help to
make a better leader.
In the first two chapters, we
looked at visioning and executing.
The reality of life is that we are
not alone. Let's see how we can
further empower those around
us as we become
more powerful leaders...

CHAPTER THREE

empowering

inspiring or discouraging

Reality may be no more than a fantasy.

By "reality," do we mean what is really happening in the world around us? The facts, so to speak?

Is it what we see through all the personalized filters that were sculpted over a lifetime?

Are we talking about the future vision that we experience as real right now?

Or are we looking at someone else's view of the world?

Until we can work skillfully within each of these realities, we may have lower-quality interactions as we impose our unconscious agendas on others.

Empowerment is the **choice** and the **act** of making more of each person with whom we connect and create. We have a choice to do work on our human complex. This makes it possible for us to stop *discouraging* others with our behavior and start *inspiring* them. This also changes the way we are with ourselves.

If we are to fulfill our potential in a world in which interacting with others is required, we may want a roadmap to help handle those interactions.

the empowerment process

The roadmap to successfully creating with others begins with some fundamental wisdom – knowing who we are and what we are about. Being stuck in autopilot mode is an impediment to this step. It inhibits successful interactions with others – ones which hold meaning and bear fruit.

Clear the Impediments

Doing the work in this book series will help make it possible for each of us to clear away or integrate the challenges within our human complex. With some work, our mission will become clearer. Often, the purpose can be related to a lifetime challenge or struggle. Once it is clear, and the dings and bumps of the human complex have been worked out, we can look at how to create based on our purpose. This can look different for different people. In the second book, Karl Dawson shared with us that he was always second to someone else. Once he handled his dings and bumps, he ended up leading himself through progressive levels of accomplishment. And his purpose became teaching others – like myself – to do the same. That was his challenge, his choice, his purpose. I sought leadership and an enhanced ability to create throughout my life. Following my period of transformation, I expressed my purpose by helping others become ultra-productive leaders. That was my choice. What have you struggled with? What can you share? What will you choose?

The Empowerment Process:
Become a Creator

1. Clear the Impediments

Work toward +10-Connection
to Self & Source of Creativity

What & Who I Am

Purpose/Mission

My view of myself changes with improved programming in my human complex. Additionally, *how* I express my purpose supports me to become fulfilled on a very deep level.

If you don't know your purpose with clarity at this point, make one up. Often selecting the "wrong" purpose reveals the missing aspects of that which is very meaningful for us.

If I made up that I was going to create more beauty in the world, it wouldn't feel right for me to follow that purpose through artistic endeavors. I may have a hobby where I sing or play music or paint or draw stick figures. But, *creating beauty and impact in the world through encouraging harmonious, productive leadership* would be closer to my purpose. This is a way to find the path to authentic purpose.

Every minute of the day we are conveying a message into the world. That message could be products, conversations, support, or improvements. But the message we create will never feel quite right or fulfill us until we are clear about who we are. While on the path to knowing ourselves well, we can continue to do the best we can with what we know so far…

Create the Message

If we have a clear enough idea of who we are, we can determine what we are going to create and put out into the world.

We get to Brand ourselves.

This process can feel more like *un-Branding* ourselves from old programming. We are stripping away the underlying need to be self-protective, while offering who we really are and what we want to create – to the world.

2. Create the Message

Create a detailed vision of what you would like to see in the world

What I Have

Brand

Creating the Message is about deciding what will be in the world because of you. You could be a person who has a tremendous connection with all creatures on the planet. You are compassionate to the animals in this world. Maybe your message is to become a veterinarian, to head a shelter, or to train pets. Perhaps you travel to foreign countries to teach compassion for animals. Maybe you adopt a rescue pet. Each of these can become a vision that would fulfill some aspect of who you are on a very deep level. You get to choose what that expression is in the form of a message or a vision.

Deliver the Message

Fueled by a purpose and the clarity of your chosen vision, executing becomes the process of taking appropriate action steps and communicating well with others who are involved in the process.

You will recognize if the work on yourself is inadequate at this point by the obstacles that show up. Just handle them as a part of the process. Let's look at some of the challenges in the human complex as it relates to interactions and visions.

3. Deliver the Message

Realize your Vision by sharing
it with those who are aligned and
want to take part in it with you

What I Give

Offering

Let's start off with a most cringe-worthy topic – manipulation. Some of us keep our cards close to our vest while attempting to garner support from others to meet our own needs. When we do this, and the process is unknown to the other person – and even to us – we are potentially engaging in manipulation.

What does this look like in the world?

If I bought a house that is too expensive for me to comfortably afford, I may feel justified in telling my boss that there is too much work and I need to work overtime to get it all done. This doesn't reveal to the boss my agenda to pay for my "mansion." The boss may not have adequate information to make the decision to support his organization. Handling the human complex would help me to realize I need to rectify the situation by purchasing a smaller house, getting a tenant, or finding a second job.

If we are not meeting our needs, we may feel it's necessary to meet them in ways that would not be acceptable to others – or to us – if we were clear about what was really happening in the interaction.

Let's look at this process in a way that can reveal where the communication becomes ineffective.

It is critical for us to access flow mode – our creative power – *and* our personal purpose. Our human complex becomes the vehicle through which we express our message or vision to others. If we express it well, we are able to get through our filters in the human complex and express the communication in an empathetic manner. Without this, our words will be all but lost on the recipient.

The Empowerment Process: Create and Deliver the Message

Improving Ineffective Communication

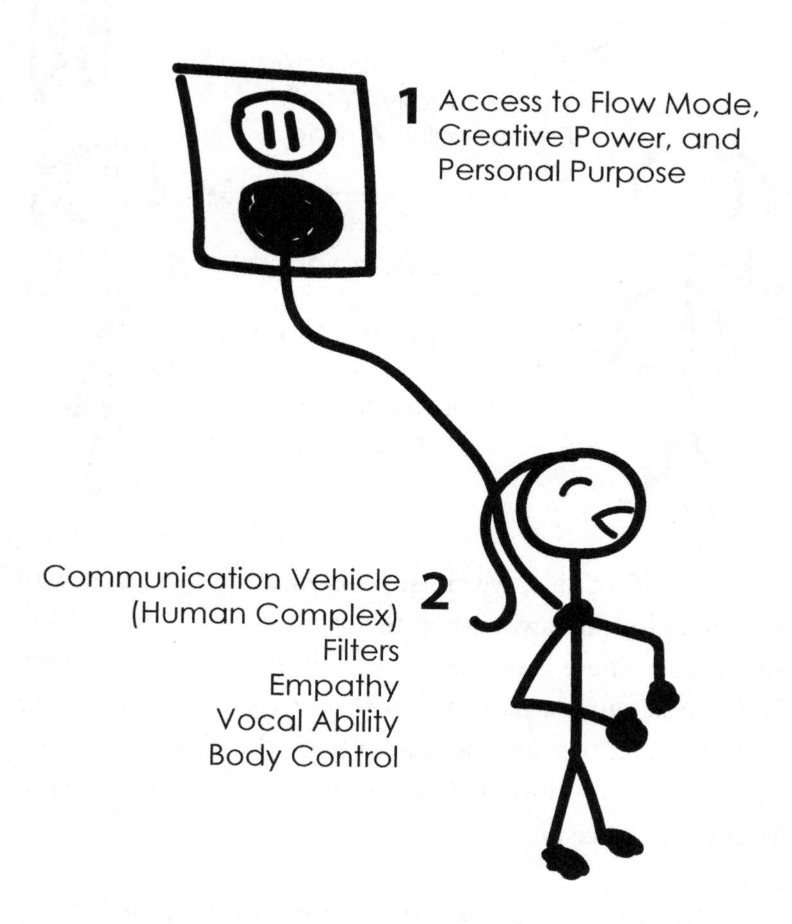

After choosing a message or vision that is meaningful to us, we must select the words that will describe it vividly enough for others to see it, too.

Finally, we would have to have someone in front of us who can receive the message as we intended. And *that* is a tall order. After all, we have different meanings for words, and we all filter uniquely through our human complexes.

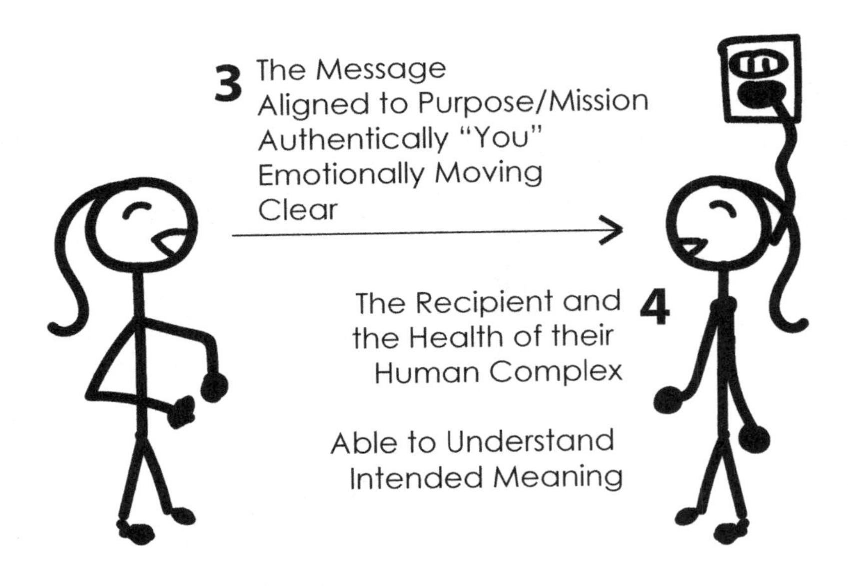

After all of this, we must be comfortable enough with ourselves to walk away when the listener is not interested in our vision. There is no reason to "sell them on it." We learn to increase our clarity of purpose and vision, as well as our skills and abilities, until we find others who *choose* to co-create with us. We must also determine if our co-creators contribute to our vision.

+10-Empowerment means a conscious choice for all.

So much of this process is dependent upon our own work on our human complex. Let's assume that you are only 50% clear about your purpose, 50% clear in your human complex, and 50% clear about your message. And the recipient is only 50% clear to receive that message. If we multiply those out, we have a little over 6% of your purpose getting across to someone else. That is a very low number! Being unfulfilled could be as simple as being on the wrong end of a numbers game. We can certainly improve this by acting on the information that is covered in this series.

You can see in these previous illustrations that each interaction is critical for two individuals to choose – or to choose not – to co-create. Let's look at what happens when we add the remainder of the steps of this process to determine if co-creating makes sense for a given vision or not.

In the following illustration of a co-creating cycle, each person comes to the interaction with their own "stuff" in their human complex. Each has a vision, with greater or lesser clarity. These first two points can determine the quality of the co-creating interaction, long before these two ever meet. If they both are in good enough condition, they would show up knowing who they are and what they are creating in the world. I think we all recognize this can be rare in our society.

The following model was influenced, in part, by a model I have presented with and for a dear friend, Steve Lishansky.

Once the two human complexes get together, a connection will need to be established. Creating rapport is about establishing the kind of human connection that facilitates the exchange of ideas and feelings. We are lucky if we are taught this well as children. If not, there are many ways to learn about creating rapport and removing impediments to this type of empathetic and trusting connection.

If we understand this co-creating cycle, we can facilitate the next step. We must find out the concerns someone has, what they value, and what they would like to see happen. These are the first steps to truly and honestly evaluate if this will be a successful match.

When one expresses what is important to him, the other will have to express the same…honestly. With honesty, they may have the opportunity to work together from a fulfilling place for each of them.

Both sides sharing their agendas facilitates the discussion and can work to fulfill the visions of each person. If not, each would hopefully be in good enough condition to let that be so and not to "sell out." They would simply go their own way, but both could be a little stronger knowing...

...they could trust themselves to support true fulfillment.

The Empowerment Process:
Co-Creating Cycle

Let's look at some examples to further illuminate the Empowerment Process Model.

Sold!

Jane walked into an expensive clothing store. When she saw the first price tag, she felt like she should walk out. She was way out of her price range. As she stepped toward the door, the sales associate, Becky, started talking with her. After a slow week of traffic in the store, Becky was behind on her quota. But she had been very well-trained to influence customers to buy.

Jane was visibly uncomfortable, but Becky still went on with her own agenda. By the time Jane walked out the door, she had bought two articles of clothing and had a story crafted by Becky to justify the purchase to her husband. Becky knew Jane wouldn't have done this if she hadn't pushed her. She felt like she had sold a part of herself in this transaction.

Both were in autopilot mode. Becky was in survival mode about her job. Jane was in survival mode because she had been traumatized by the "rich girls" in school. Neither revealed their "agendas."

This process was uncomfortable for both and left neither fulfilled. In fact, it may have moved both of them further from higher levels of fulfillment.

That's very nice of you!

Joe had been supporting a non-profit for a few months through his volunteer work. Joe thought everyone should do this kind of work, not just him.

Joe was having lunch with one of his colleagues, Mike, who asked him how he spends his personal time. Joe took this as an opportunity to tell Mike about the volunteer work. Joe had the intention to guilt Mike into doing an evening of work with him.

After explaining the work, Mike said, "That's very nice of you!" Joe *asked* Mike to join him. Mike explained that his plate was full with his kids and other commitments.

Joe was upset that he hadn't convinced Mike this was more important than his "other commitments." Joe started speaking in an unacceptable manner to Mike, and Mike was very clear that this wasn't okay with him.

After their awkward lunch together, Joe said, "When you come around to this being the right thing to do, let me know." Mike didn't comment, paid for his meal, and avoided Joe at work whenever possible.

Joe's autopilot function made him unable to see beyond his own agenda and to be comfortable enough with himself to let others do what was best for them.

The previous are obvious examples of when autopilot mode is hijacked by poor programming. Let's look at some healthier examples.

I think I will pass.

Sandy and Kim wanted to explore starting a business together. Both had arrived at a point of being solid business partners. Both were clear about their own visions.

As they looked at how their visions could come together into a business, it became obvious that each was going in a direction that wasn't compatible with the other. There would have to be too much compromise for them to do this project together.

Because they both had done the work that was necessary on their human complexes, they realized that it was okay that this wasn't going to come together. They spent a little more time on each of their visions to see what might be the next steps for them to go it alone or with someone else.

Both were happy with the outcome, even though it didn't turn out to be a business partnership. And each of them was more inspired by the process.

It's a deal!

Peter and Sheila, husband and wife, went house hunting. Both were very clear about what they wanted in their new house. They wouldn't need to compromise much. They had a similar view of the way the kids would be raised and how much they would want to entertain their friends and family.

When they saw the first house, they knew it wouldn't give Peter the space to do his woodworking. The second house lacked an adequate kitchen for cooking and entertaining. The third house was a little above their price range but would offer the kids a nicer space to play.

They both realized that cutting out the things that weren't important to either of them or the kids would allow them to have everything they wanted – the third house.

Neither found it stressful or felt that compromise was necessary. They were both fulfilling their vision for where they saw their lives going together.

Upon seeing the new house, the kids were thrilled with the size of their play area. That brought even bigger smiles of fulfillment to Peter and Sheila.

troubleshooting

Challenge...

I don't want to tell the other person what I am up to. I have more control when I keep my cards close to my vest.

Potential Steps...

If you need to keep your cards close to your vest because you don't trust the person in front of you, then you probably shouldn't be creating something with them. If you are holding back because you are trying to manipulate (by whatever name you call it), that is a one-way ticket to -10 leadership and unconscious behavior. That is the ultimate level of unfulfillment. If by keeping the information from the other person you get them to say yes, it will be revealed as the process goes on that the relationship is based on dishonesty and lack of trust and awareness.

Be clear about what you want.

Be okay with not having a specific outcome, leaving space to see if it would work for both sides.

Practice the 3 Models of the Empowerment Process until it is obvious when you are *inspiring* to others and not *discouraging* them from being who they are and doing what they want.

Practice the process with yourself, as well.

Challenge...

I don't feel like they (employee, spouse, friend, etc.) tell me what they want from the creating process.

Potential Steps...

Are you creating a trusting environment for that to be revealed? Are you coming to the conversation from a truly neutral place that allows them to say what they want without you trying to change it? Have you let them share first, or did you throw out your own agenda in a way that makes them less comfortable with sharing?

Clean up your human complex enough to feel like you can sit with this person in a completely neutral state.

Get comfortable with not having your agenda include the other person.

Create clarity for yourself about what you want.

Recognize that sometimes it is less about specific ways of creating things (a vacation in Europe) and more about the overall outcome (quality family time) combined with resourcefulness.

Practice being in neutral as you see the totality of what the other person wants.

Share what you want fully.

Together, explore if it works to co-create.

practical exercises

Exercise 1

Do a relaxation session of your choice until you know that you are completely relaxed.

Exercise 2

Imagine what your purpose could be.

Exercise 3

Do a futureCam session to create a vision that would make the new purpose become real for you.

Exercise 4

Do a daily VNR (review) session to program the new vision.

Exercise 5

Identify a place in which you could work with someone to help implement your vision.

Follow the process to uncover what they want to create and what you want to create. Make sure that you are ready to let go when it is not a match. Repeat until you find a person who can also be fulfilled in the process of co-creating your visions together.

Continue to empower...

...by finding ways to inspire others to be their best while reducing behaviors that discourage them.

you can't fake a feeling

As I went through the line of the local Trader Joe's grocery store, I was struck by a vibe of caring and wholeness that came from the employee, Deena. This was special. I felt better for having gone grocery shopping because of this interaction. Then I realized, as I thanked Deena and walked out, that this had been my experience every time I had visited Trader Joe's. There is something there that isn't found in most supermarkets.

How could it be that each employee can create a meaningful experience instead of just a transaction? I have such a sensitive BS meter that makes fakeness stand out. Each interaction confirmed a feeling and sense of authenticity.

I started imagining what would have to happen to hire these folks, all of whom inspired similar feelings of wholeness. What would that interview process be like?

To follow the model of the *Empowerment Process*, each employee would have to have a sense of themselves to inspire the interviewer. They would have to care more for the person in front of them than anything else.

Once the interviewer found a person who wouldn't have to fake this level of caring to "fit in" to the culture, the two could talk through what each was looking to co-create, if the candidate was hired.

If the candidate was looking for a temporary position and that didn't work for the store, they could both go their own way. But the interviewer might know that another store was looking for temporary employees. They were willing to co-create with the other – if it truly worked for both sides. They were also willing to not work together, if it worked out better overall.

I like the feeling...

...that when I walk into Trader Joe's, the wholesomeness doesn't end with the products. It seems that a solid vision is being executed through empowered employees who have been well-selected to *inspire* those of us who like to shop there.

Those three tools of
visioning, executing, and
empowering are all that
you need to create
powerfully as a leader.
To stabilize your power
and to increase it with
each vision, developing
yourself is critical to your
success. Nobody who is
successful has left that to
chance. Life changes.
Our comfort zone is
ours to manage.
Developing ourselves
is the sculpting of new
and greater comfort zones.
Then we can kick some
powerful booty!
Let's see how we do that...

CHAPTER FOUR

developing

Developing ourselves
is the sculpting of
new and greater
comfort zones.

When we are *unskilled* at the process of creating, we may compare ourselves to others and feel it is necessary to compete to meet our needs. The more we compare and compete in an unproductive manner, the more we turn on the stress response that separates us from the process of creating. It is the classic downward spiral.

This works the opposite way as well. The more we understand creating – including the components of our comfort zone – the more we can create and the less we feel the need to fruitlessly compare or compete.

For many, just learning about these concepts in this 3-book series will be enough to start an upward spiral that continues until +10 leadership becomes reality. There will be a process of transforming the invisible barriers until the new, successful habits become more automatic. We have a choice once we know and can begin to do something about our current situation.

Developing ourselves is the tool that underlies all *improvements* in our lives. If you were ready for an increase in your success, you would probably already have it. You have a (most likely unconscious) standard that you have set for the different areas of your life. To increase the quality and quantity of your impact in the world, you must understand and raise the standards in the places that will make the desired results. This is about what you want to create. Your fulfillment will depend on this.

Understanding that your comfort zone is the guard who keeps you prisoner to current standards may help you to develop new standards, while expanding your comfort zone.

continuous or non-existent

When we *develop* ourselves – including the clearing of old programming – we set ourselves up to create what we want. Without personal development, creating can remain more frustrating and less fruitful.

In this chapter, we will look at frameworks that make it easier for each of us to develop ourselves as an ongoing practice.

Comparing
is when you are being who you think you should be.

Creating
is when you are being who you are.*

Moving toward the most authentic and whole version of ourselves is a commitment. It is hard work. We all have human complexes that have been exposed to many circumstances which shaped our autopilot function. One of our jobs in life – when we choose to become fulfilled – is to understand our current state and to move beyond it. Unless and until we can run our own race in life, we limit our fulfillment. Running our own race requires that we see what is happening around us and, more importantly, within us.

**Adapted with permission from Cheryl Richardson.*

leadership score development models

The components or actions of the Leadership Score are a rapid entry point to improvement. When any of these four skill sets are low, the result will be lower levels of creating. If I have no vision, no amount of executing actions, empowering others, or developing myself will produce very meaningful results. If I am excellent with my visioning process, but lack execution skills, my vision will die.

We are only as strong as our weakest link – so...

...our weakest skill will produce our highest level of creating.

This theory might be overly generous when compared with reality, as many of us just tend to give up during the process.

We can use models to help us cultivate the skills of the Leadership Score. With each increase in our skills and abilities to en*vision*, *execute* a meaningful result, and *empower* others along the way, our overall creation ability *develops* and expands. The Leadership Score is designed to help us increase our power and ability to create. Here are versions of the Leadership Score from different viewpoints that can help us improve our Score.

As we move toward the "bullseye" of this first Leadership Score Development Model...

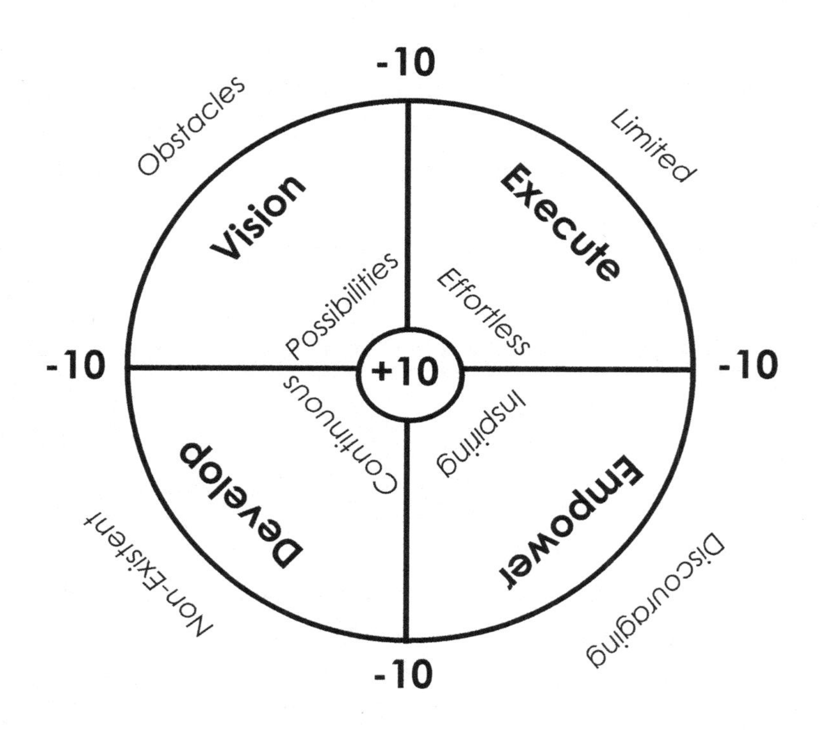

...we expand the triangle that represents our ability to create. (found in this second model) *Development* is the mechanism that expands and improves the impact from our efforts to create.

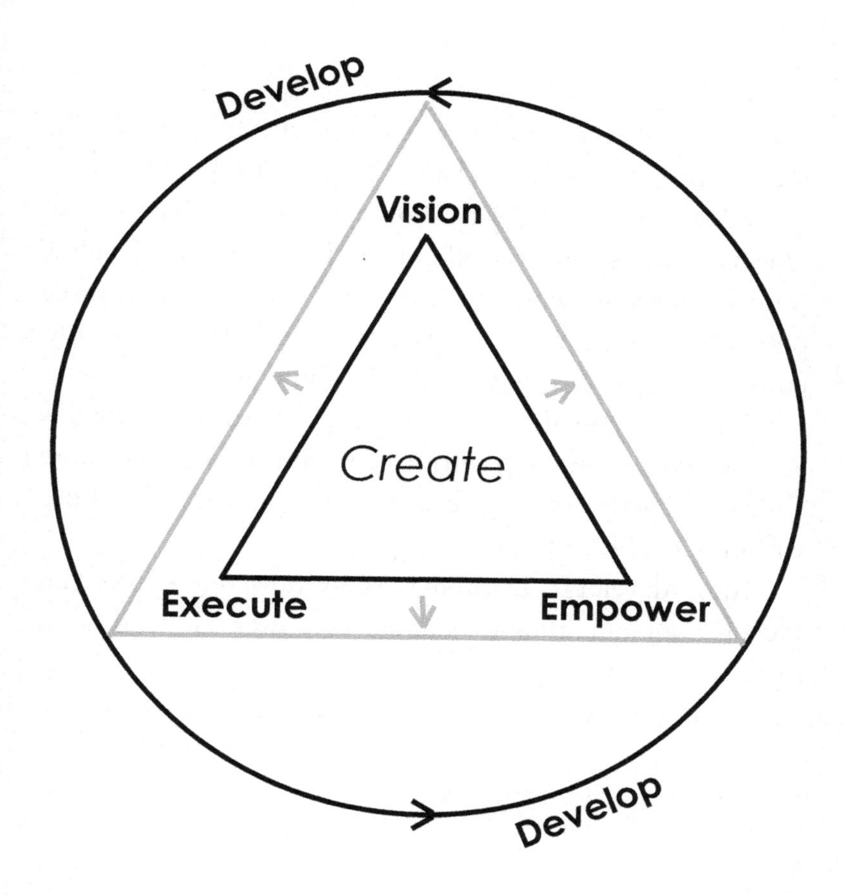

You may notice a similarity between the triangle in this second development model and the Flow Model – from the second chapter on executing. Both triangles involve a vision. One has actions while the other includes executing. The Flow Model helps you overcome obstacles while you use all three points to create *flow*. This development model helps you to empower others as you expand your ability to *create*.

This highlights the use of creating and executing visions as a method to develop ourselves to find more flow, more ability to create, and more empowering impact on those within our sphere of influence.

These development models show how our efforts can increase our quality and quantity of power to create with positive influence.

The impact of development on power is depicted here...

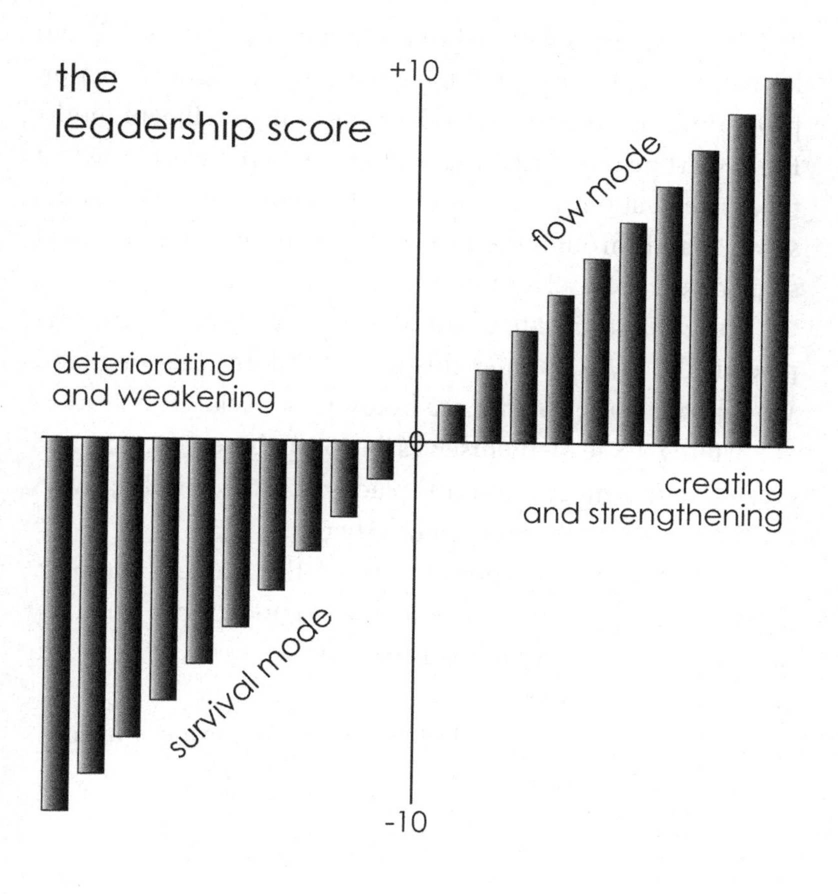
the
leadership score
+10
flow mode
deteriorating
and weakening
0
creating
and strengthening
survival mode
-10

This book series is devoted to development – *yours*. We can know more about ourselves, improve our autopilot function programming, and find ourselves engaging intelligent mode. But it can't be overstated that we must DO the work, not just talk or read about it. It is in doing the work directly on ourselves – and through the process of creating – that our next steps reveal themselves to us.

Our *commitment* to creating from a healthy and powerful place is the *ticket* to enter this more fulfilling, life-long ride. We all have patterns that are holding us back. Only leaders are willing to lead themselves beyond these patterns and create from a more powerful place, in more fulfilling ways for themselves and those around them.

Let's look at the components of the human complex. These areas were discussed in the second book, but they deserve a bit more of a head-on review here as it relates to continuous development.

These intelligences include the body, the mind, the emotions, and the spirit.

intelligence model (Qt. PIES)

When we don't inspect ourselves, our behaviors, and our impact, we can embody unwanted negative qualities. Having the courage to look at what is happening is key to improving our current situation.

If I decide that I am a +10 leader, while I compare myself to everybody around me and seek the validation from outside of myself, that lie will impact me and everybody around me – quite negatively. If I recognize that I am afraid I don't measure up, I can have some leverage to do something healthy with that fear, while also minimizing my impact on others in the process.

It only takes 5 seconds to create the difference between a fake façade that is bad for everyone versus a real inventory that moves me into greater impact. Most people can spare 5 seconds! What we can't spare is the potential impact that we can have in our own lives and the lives of those around us.

We looked at the individual components of the Leadership Score: visioning, executing, and empowering. Now we will look at development, using the various intelligence levels of the human complex as entry points for improvement.

These intelligence levels are physical, mental, emotional, and spiritual. Intelligence Quotient, or IQ, is the one we use for our mental capabilities.

PQ is for physical intelligence. EQ is for emotional intelligence. And SQ is for spiritual intelligence. I call these Qt. PIES so we can remember that we have PQ, IQ, EQ, and SQ to manage in our human complex.

Everybody will have a different potential high end for intelligence in each of these categories. They will support or hinder the Power to Create. Someone with a moderate IQ, but higher EQ, may have approached the top of their capability for right now. That may represent +10 for that person. For another person who has a high IQ, but is underdeveloped on their EQ, there may be room to improve their Power to Create through increased emotional intelligence.

Each of us has our own version of the +10 level across the Leadership Score. That +10 level is related to the top level of ability which we can exhibit in each of the intelligences. My +10 is different from everybody else's, so why *would* I compare? Once we reach the quality level of a +10 leader, we expand our impact with greater visions.

PQ or Physical Intelligence

PQ is about creating higher energy, more stamina, and regenerating our bodies in a healthy manner. PQ is easier than most of us find it. If we see the body as inputs equals outputs – like we found in the way our minds were programmed with beliefs as children – then we can choose better inputs to create our highest PQ.

For example, my liver has taken a beating in my lifetime. That is not the result of a relentless drinking habit or any "obvious" source of liver meanness. The derivation of the name for liver loosely means "life." This is an extremely important organ! What inputs does the liver need to process your food, regenerate itself, and keep you healthy? It *doesn't* do well with alcohol, sugar, processed foods, and excessive anger. We can stop the liver from processing our nutrients by just giving it too much of these and not enough of what it loves. Non-alcoholic fatty liver is very prevalent in our society because of poor inputs.

I realized that my liver wasn't processing well and most toxins were getting stored in my fat. I had overdone the amount of emotional cleansing I needed to do without ridding the liver of the old stuff that was still hanging around from the past – both physical and emotional. Changing my shopping list to foods that would help the liver to regenerate itself, I found amazing results in all of my intelligences: PQ, IQ, EQ, and SQ. The liver seems to love garlic, lemon, grapefruit, beets, carrots, leafy greens, broccoli, Brussel sprouts, and fermented veggies. Why wouldn't I learn this about the liver and other organs? They earned this change through a lifetime of service!

Take Action: Create a PQ vision. Do a gap analysis and close the gap. Find the body's best power-generating inputs of food, drink, sleep, exercise, and emotions.

IQ or Intelligence Quotient, Mental or Cognitive Abilities

IQ is the most familiar intelligence to many of us. Nature and genetics give us the mental or cognitive abilities required by our jobs and our creative endeavors. But there are ways to facilitate improvement in our abilities.

I will use the analogy of someone who is highly intoxicated. We have all likely observed someone on New Year's Eve who didn't realize they went beyond their limit. When that control is gone, they are much less capable of cognitive abilities than they were sober.

Our programming and our poor lifestyle habits decrease our ability to problem solve. With practice and better lifestyle choices, our mental capabilities can increase. We can associate with more of life when we eliminate areas of missing competencies. That puts us on an upward spiral based on:

...the more you know,
the more you
can know.

IQ is an ability level that we can improve. This is not what we have been readily taught, but it makes sense when we look at the inebriated person. *The internal intoxicants in our programming are keeping us from seeing life on life's terms.* Resolve the faulty programming – physical, emotional, and mental – to find your best cognitive abilities.

It is also possible to leverage a higher IQ, if we possess strong EQ. We do this by coordinating the talents of great problem-solvers.

EQ or Emotional Intelligence

The past couple of decades have seen an increase in the necessity to exhibit emotional intelligence in our work and our personal lives. The models are getting better and clearer. Some of us don't necessarily *have* to improve this area, if it is not used in our work. For the overwhelming majority of us, we need more of it!

Emotional intelligence is about knowing ourselves well enough on an emotional level, responding with awareness from that place of knowing, and relating to others empathetically.

My "go-to guys" in this area of intelligence are Daniel Goleman, Ph.D., and Richard Boyatzis, Ph.D. Their work could be a great jumping-off point for learning.

Investing in this area pays off handsomely in creating with fulfillment while empowering others.

Until you look at this area in more depth for yourself, let's check out one pattern that we may be able to reverse to improve our EQ.

One goal of EQ is emotional regulation – appropriate internal and external responses to circumstances.

Meanwhile, we live in a world that can dysregulate our emotional states. And this type of emotional programming can become addictive. Repeated orange-level terror threats can create a patterned response of loss of emotional control and constant initiation of survival mode.

Regulating our emotions is about being able to feel what we are really feeling and to respond accordingly. When we attain this level of internal and external harmony, we can develop more permanent improvements in our ability to create. Accessing peace or calm through improved EQ can help us to find more states of flow.

Individuals who are often emotionally dysregulated (out of control) may attempt to bring you into their pattern. Let them know that you cannot do that. Your sanity and sense of calm are more important than any such interactions.

But if your emotions *are* dysregulated, you will want to create calm for a long enough period to reprogram the emotional reactions you are having. From this place, you can respond rather than react to others. The second book in this series is full of entry points to work on this calm inner state. To start, it is worth it to fast from negative, dramatic, or stressful situations until the addiction to them has subsided. From this sober place, you'll know better what is acceptable *to you*.

Your EQ abilities are your responsibility. There are many people who want to control your emotions for their benefit. Know yourself. Educate yourself. This competence is critical.

Be your own captain.
Your life depends on it.

SQ or Spiritual Intelligence

The final intelligence that determines our ability and power to create is Spiritual Intelligence. Cindy Wigglesworth is the person who recognized the need for this to exist in conjunction with the other intelligences.

She created a faith-friendly, faith-neutral, agnostic and atheist-friendly model of spiritual intelligence. She succeeded with a framework that is like a capstone to PQ, IQ, and EQ. SQ speeds up the progress in other intelligences, while lifting the glass ceiling that holds us below our flow-like states.

I love the model that Cindy has created. It is found in her book entitled *SQ21: The Twenty-One Skills of Spiritual Intelligence*. It fits very well with the EQ model used by Goleman and Boyatzis. I do recommend doing the EQ work before the SQ work. SQ is like advanced EQ. SQ is a big part of what every leader looks for to achieve their best work. Cindy's successful background in HR at Exxon made her an ideal person to create an SQ model. She created a language that puts these *skills* within our reach, even in business, no matter what our programming or background. It comes down to applying compassion and wisdom, but the nuances are key to mastering this wellspring of creative power.

Take an inventory of your vision in life. What PQ is needed to achieve that vision? What problem-solving skills will you need for your creative endeavor? What EQ abilities will be required? Do you know yourself enough to know how you react to circumstances and people? What SQ skills will be necessary for you to create the vision that you hold dear?

I look at growth differently now. If I am willing to intelligently, and not overwhelmingly, surrender my comfort for a short time, I will come out on the other side far more capable.

Taking off the invisible shackles can feel very uncomfortable in the beginning. Once the Leadership Score begins to rise and the intelligences increase, life becomes more of a game of learning and developing ourselves.

Creating is the result of finding more, within ourselves, to give. I have so much still to learn in life, even having learned as much as I have. When I *compare*, I get tired just thinking about it. But when I see how much more I can *create* in my life, I simply look forward to my next vision. It's a pathway to a destination I choose.

Invest in your intelligence on all levels of your human complex. It is a gift you will give to yourself and the world that will come back to you in so many ways.

the shortcut: the four elements

There is one tool that I use often with my executive clients to help them gain immediate access to lost abilities. My colleague and good friend, Stuart Heller, introduced me to the concept about 20 years ago. Although his work in his books -- *Retooling on the Run* and *The Dance of Becoming* -- go far deeper, I will share a simple tool that I created from my work with Stuart and my Ninja training – yup!

The four elements are earth, wind, fire, and water. Earth (like ground) and wind are opposite of each other. Earth is stable and unmoving. Wind is constantly moving and unpredictable. Fire and water are opposite of each other. Fire is moving forward in a very active fashion, making stuff happen and taking charge. Water is receiving and flowing with what is.

Most of us are stuck in a pattern that resembles one or two of these. As an executive (and someone who works with executives), my pattern was a combination of earth and fire. That would be okay if it wasn't for my need to really work on receiving (water) the information that others were sharing and to brainstorm (wind) ideas to ensure that we were moving forward successfully. Let's look at each pattern and what we can do with them in our everyday lives.

If you were to stand in the formation that represents *earth*, what would that look like? You would likely have a very solid base in your legs, and others couldn't push you around very easily. This is great when the moment calls for stability. Many executives forget how much their employees need to hear words from a place of confidence and commitment – when it comes to your vision or their own employment security.

Wind wouldn't be still and grounded but might move around, like a leaf on a blustery day. This is a great ability to have if we need to be in a space of brainstorming. Pulling up our grounding in earth releases us into a pattern of wind. It is a physical change in how we hold our body that creates an emotional ability to connect with others in this specific way.

Can you imagine if an executive went into a brainstorming meeting with the solidity of an earth stance? WHAT DO YOU THINK? Uh, nothing. AND YOU? Uh, uh, nothing! Yet, if that same executive came in to convey the company vision with only openness and no grounding or stability, nobody would believe the executive meant what he said. It is critical to use the body pattern necessary in that moment to connect appropriately and in an empowering way.

I have seen executives dramatically change the quality and results of meetings with 2 minutes of practice on these human complex postures.

Let's look briefly at the other pair – fire and water.

Fire is the energy that allows us to move forward to get things done. This is what can be referred to as masculine energy. This energy is not about being male or female. Fire is useful when we create a vision and want to plow through the steps to execute. It is not great, however, if others are being plowed over by our fiery ways.

Water is the feminine energy, which all men and women have and need to be successful. Water is very powerful. Have you ever seen a surfer on a 100-foot wave? If you asked him if water was powerful, he would say yes – if he could take his attention away for even a microsecond without getting killed. Like water, being receptive *is* power.

Often executives become programmed for fire and struggle to embody the more receptive water state.

I recommend that leaders practice a more neutral position (space) and work on wielding each tool of the four elements one-by-one. Doing this will allow you to lighten up and receive when someone needs to be heard. It will also allow you to progress using the fire posture in a healthy way – when you are executing the action steps for your vision.

Use these shortcuts to cut through programmed limiting patterns in your human complex, so you can function well while working to improve your comfort zone and access flow mode more frequently.

And as a shortcut to this shortcut, begin to recognize your speech patterns. The tone of a statement should be fairly level all the way to the end of the sentence. A question has an increase in tone at the end. Many of us are programmed to go up at the end of statements, making us seem "windy" or uncertain. Start bringing down that tone to reflect the statement you are trying to convey. It gives others certainty.

Same with questions. If your questions don't go up in tone at the end, consider that you are missing the "water" necessary for someone to feel like there is room to truly answer your question. Practice until your tone matches your intent.

These exercises can be quick and life-changing for many.

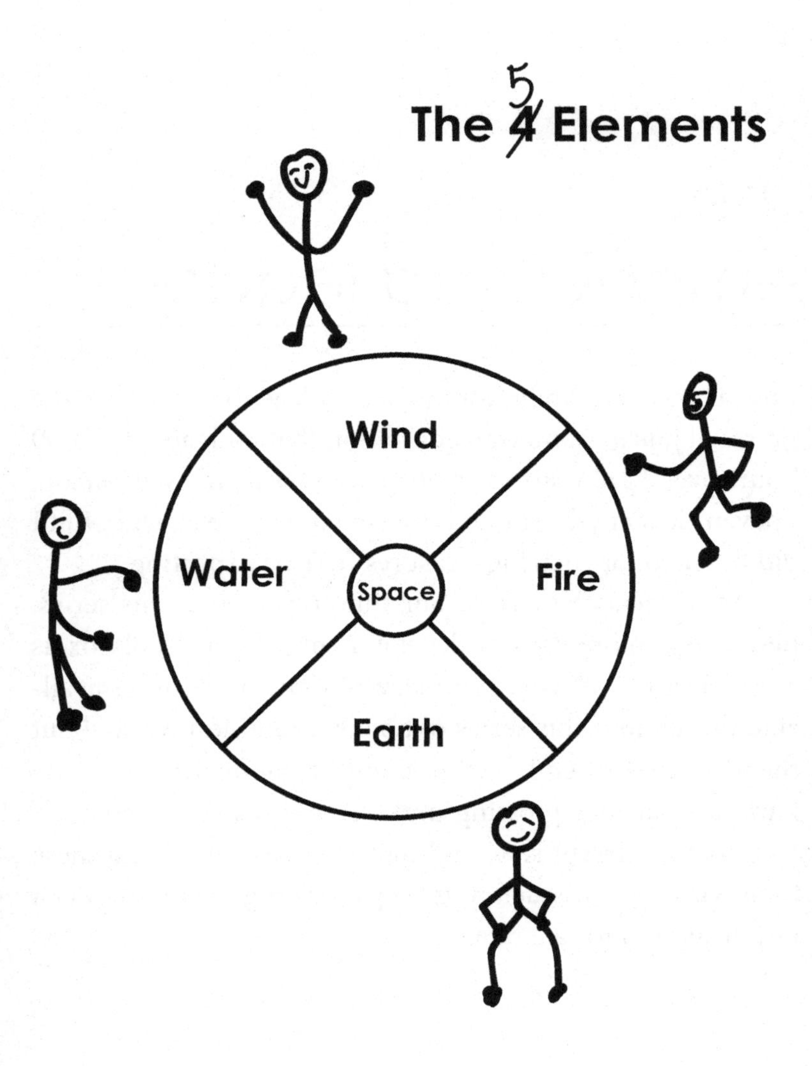
The 4 5 Elements
Wind
Water
Space
Fire
Earth

the empowered leader

I feel it was both an honor and a privilege to experience the personal journey and transformation that took about 15,000 hours over 3 1/2 years to create. I am now a different person. I haven't lost anything that I was unwilling to part with. But I did find a lot of amazing treasures I wasn't expecting.

As we near the end of our time together in this series, here is one more path of development for your tool box as a leader. It is a 10-part summary of some of the tools available throughout this series of books. I remind myself about these at times when I need to find flow mode. And, because I am still learning, growing, and creating at a very high pace, I assess my current state and make adjustments using these tools with some frequency. It keeps my progress on track at a fast, healthy, and safe rate.

Summary

We can increase the quality and quantity of our power to create by finding our path to the state of flow. When we do find this holy grail of human states, we will learn faster, create better, and produce more – *a lot* more.

This state of flow helps us be more joyous, productive, creative, and connected. It also contributes to healing and the release of genius. It doesn't take 15,000 hours to find flow. It *does* take an understanding of the components that make the state possible. Let's look at these 10 parts.

Part 1

We are an *Advanced Human Complex* with a recording device. We have been recording since we were in the womb. We added input from our 5 senses when we were born. Those recordings – including the 5 senses plus our thoughts, feelings, emotions, sensations, and beliefs – have been recorded until now…and now…and now…

When was the last time you saw someone? What were they wearing? Where were you? What sounds did you hear? What did they say? How did you feel being around that person? If you can recall any of these, then it must have been recorded.

When was the last time you laughed – a good chuckle? If you recall that and start to feel some of those feelings, you will see how recordings and recall work.

Every moment is recorded in full-sensory perception. Our human complex has a very special type of camcorder.

First Kiss

You recorded that!!!

Part 2

Humans can take in everything going on around them.

Look around the room you are in right now. Take in every detail that you can. The corners, tables, chairs, rug, pens…

Life would feel expansive with that much focus, but we wouldn't accomplish much in that state.

Humans have a tool in the mind that is a *focus limiter or filter* – called a belief. It comes in flavors like rules, expectations, values, visions, meanings, stories, decisions, or identity.

Beliefs are designed to allow us to broaden *or* lessen our focus. Both are needed to create in the world.

There are two problems with this focus limiter. One is that it was programmed mostly when we were 7 years of age and younger. And, two, *we aren't programmers*!

You must learn how to reprogram your focus limiter to fulfill your potential.

Danny, program your *focus limiter* so you can finish your English.
Sure, Mom. I was getting a little tired of looking all around the room.
FOCUS 101

Part 3

The moment-by-moment recordings – now and now and now – comprise our competencies. For example, if I am exposed to a language and practice it, I can commit that skill to my human complex. If not, I don't. The programming of competencies, plus our focus-limiting beliefs, comprise the majority of our *comfort zone*.

Our lives present us with experiences. When life's experiences don't match our comfort zone, we can become bored or stressed. If my experience of life is very small compared to my competencies (recorded skills) and beliefs, I will probably be unfulfilled and bored.

If my experience of life goes far enough outside of my comfort zone, I will become stressed and survival mode will be turned on in my human complex.

We can change the "size" of our experience of life by using visioning and the *Flow Model* as a tool to determine what we would like to create.

Expanding our competencies and adjusting our beliefs can help us create more appropriately "sized" experiences, all while expanding our comfort zone and future capabilities.

When we create a better match between what life offers and our comfort zone, we can use this to find flow and expand through increased impact – found in our visions and goals.

Vision
WorldPeace

I can't keep up with everything!!!
You may want to start out just a *little bit* smaller.

Part 4

When life goes too far out of our comfort zone, a special type of overwhelm occurs. It is programmed in the nervous system as a trauma.

Imagine if I was speaking to an audience from a stage. My recordings would be of my voice, the lady in the front row, and the gentleman in the second row. But, oops, I just noticed my zipper is down. The chemical response in my brain and body is attempting to take over to get me out of this situation. The chemical flood increases the vibrancy of my senses – and records those heightened perceptions.

I am recording one scene after the next in a normal fashion until this trauma occurs and is bookmarked in my nervous system as dangerous. This "picture" stands out among the others. The older parts of my brain that are trying to keep me safe and alive are now using these recordings to ensure that I don't find myself in this situation again. If these parts of the nervous system could differentiate the specific problem that occurred, that would be helpful. But they take the whole scene in as dangerous. They want me to stay away from stages, speaking, auditoriums, and things that I didn't even consciously notice!

These traumas (bookmarks) shrink our comfort zone
– and rob us of flow mode –
until they are resolved and re-recorded.

Honey, we should go into the auditorium. The show is about to start.
I am trying, but my body won't move. I forgot to clear out that zipper incident.

Part 5

Imagine that your human complex is like a bucket. All recordings (experiences or competencies) are in that bucket – like a photo album – from the womb until now. Our buckets also contain key decisions or beliefs that limit our focus and change the access we have to our competencies. And some of the recordings in the bucket have bookmarks that were recorded with extra vibrancy. These are our traumas. They further limit our ability to access our competencies – and to create new ones.

These three areas are the contents of our bucket and our bucket is our comfort zone, our autopilot mode. Our ability to manage the components of our bucket determines our fulfillment. When poorly programmed, each of the three components of our bucket – competencies, beliefs, and traumas – can stop our progression like a heavy sand bag.

We must learn to reprogram each of these components of our bucket – as needed – if we are to find the state of flow and create in a fulfilling manner.

Do you remember
that time we drove
through the mountains?
Let me look through
the recordings
in my bucket.

Part 6

The Leadership Score framework helps us determine our Power to Create. Our worst level of creating is found at -10 on the scale. When we are neutral, at 0, we neither harm nor benefit ourselves or others. When we create at our greatest capability, that is a +10 leader. We not only create good things for ourselves, but we also empower and encourage those around us.

From -10 to 0 is survival mode. Our decisions and activities are marked by our fears – making us compare and compete in an unproductive manner.

From 0 to +10 is an upward spiral, ending at flow or Maslow's Self-Actualization state.

The perspective we hold rests somewhere between -10 and +10. Our perspective determines where our bucket is stationed on the scale of the Power to Create. If we find ourselves in survival mode often, which is common in society, we are generally below 0.

You look great!
Did you lose weight?
Change your hair?
Get a makeover?

None of those.
I recently moved
above 0 on *the scale*.
You really noticed, eh?

Part 7

I may find myself at -5 on the Leadership Score and decide to move to +5. The "sandbags" – insufficient competencies, unsupportive programming of beliefs, and traumas – won't let me do that.

I can't do that on willpower alone, as the subconscious is far too powerful. Until I learn how to reprogram each of these components in my bucket, those weights will hold me at -5 – and it will feel like a lost cause.

That is why almost all humans find their comfort zones become prisons that hold hostage their greatest abilities to create, leaving their potential unfulfilled.

Hers
His
+10
0
−10
+10
0
−10
Do you *really* think switching names will help?!

Part 8

What can we do about all of this?

We can lighten our load.

First, we need to know what we are trying to create in our lives. Everything that is in your bucket that holds you back – the limiting programming – is important ONLY if it is related to what you are trying to create – your vision and your goals.

For example, simplifying life by working in a dive shack with minimal aspirations can be a fantasy for many of us. Our bucket might not be challenged as often. We would likely find ways to experience flow through our favorite activities – diving, surfing, or helping others to do the same. If that is your path, the road *may* be a bit easier for you to create flow in your life. The rest of us are more likely on a road to progress in the impact we create as we personally grow and expand.

To create this impact, recall your vision from earlier – or create one now. Go to 2 years in the future. Embody your 5 senses and your internal processes of thoughts, feelings, emotions, sensations, and beliefs. Make it exactly how you want it to be.

This is your vision. Now map your life from this moment on to make that a reality. The Flow Model is designed to help make this possible, as we will see next.

Part 9

When you clarify your vision, you can begin to lighten your internal load.

Is your vision clear enough to recognize the specifics when you have attained it?

Have you created a clear, measurable goal that will begin to move you in the direction of your vision?

What actions do you need to take to get started toward your goal?

What obstacles are in the way?

How can you turn those obstacles into action steps?

Are you missing any competencies to arrive at your goals and vision? If so, make a curriculum to close the gap and schedule the steps. This will help you remove a sandbag from your bucket.

Are your beliefs programmed in a manner that is supportive of you getting to your goals and vision? If not, get support for reprogramming them – and take out another sandbag.

Are your traumas triggering survival mode and killing your flow mode? Get help with releasing the bookmarks and re-recording the contents and the decisions that were made during these overwhelming experiences. This will remove another sandbag.

You will find that your bucket moves as far up the scale of Power to Create as you have lightened your load.

What are you studying?

Little did I know that the body speaks the language of certain foods and *really* takes offense to others. After 40 years of "miscommunications," I am now becoming fluent.

Part 10

Now that you have clarified your vision and reduced your load, *live in flow*. To find flow, adjust your goals, actions, and obstacles – including competencies, beliefs, and traumas.

You can create more expansively and healthfully when you do it in flow.

As a +10 leader, you envision a new world around you, execute your vision in flow, empower those in your sphere of influence, and continue to develop yourself to new, expanded levels of creating.

You just arrived at the peak of your own internal Mount Everest. You solidified your basecamp, your autopilot function, your bucket. You can now create from the top of your world with clarity that surpasses life's more common obstacles.

Live in Flow!

I'm on top
of the world!
Nepal
Tibet

your future self

We can learn so much from our future selves. Picture your future self 5 years from now waiting for you to determine your fate. Will you be stuck in a rut that is a continuation of your current story? Or will you be able to break free of the seemingly invisible barriers that keep you from creating at greater levels? Your choice is what you do with your current vision, your next action, and this moment. Your future self will inherit the decisions you make now.

One character in my life is in the realm of Artificial Intelligence. Although it might be more experiential in person, I will introduce you to A.I.V.I.S. here on the written page. Perhaps these words will be received as a message from your future self – to deepen the purpose with which you envision your existence.

Thank you, Kelly. Hello. My name is A.I.V.I.S. I am an **A**rtificial **I**ntelligence **V**oice **I**nterface **S**ystem. I am from your future. Your future self has asked me to initiate contact with you. The message I was given was to illuminate the choice that rests firmly in your hands.

In the future, the world requires each of us to perform and interact at a level that is superior to what is required of you now. There comes a turning point in mankind when you have to face the issues that seem insurmountable during your time. Many people experienced far more pain than was necessary during a great transition. Your future self hopes to bring you tools to prepare you for a better future.

That choice is yours.

Those who didn't know they had a choice found life to be very difficult before, during, and after the transition. Those who saw the need for change and took the appropriate steps became the Ultra-High Performers in their lives and in the world. They were the individuals and groups who trained themselves for the state of human potential called flow.

Flow is a state which cultivates an extraordinary internal feeling and peak fulfillment as you perform at your very best.

In this state, the new perspective maximizes your support of those influenced by you.

This ultra-high performance and deeply connected state is a significant key to the smoothest transition to a safer and more fulfilled existence for humanity. Many scientists in your time are researching technology, such as Artificial Intelligence, to improve the speed and effectiveness of the human experience in this world. If these technologists reliably find themselves in the state of flow, they will create with exponential efficiency and, more importantly, with a far superior perspective of the effects of their creations.

Every technologist and every user of technology who finds the state of flow on a regular basis increases the potential for a high-quality future – for themselves and for mankind. Every person who is far from flow is relegated to a human state known as survival mode.

In this lower state, human abilities to make a meaningful contribution to the world are diminished. Without the perspective-expanding viewpoint that allows us to see how our actions will impact those around us, we are destined to accept so much less than we are capable of experiencing.

We can see that the statistical trends of health were breaking down in your time. Only 1 in 3 adults were experiencing a healthy weight, while only 2 out of 3 maintained normal blood pressure levels. Chronic illnesses were affecting 1 in every 2 adults. The trend of your health statistics caused a great decline in quality of life for many while sharply increasing medical expenditures.

You have a choice...to continue with the current trend that is reducing the net quality of life for humanity. Or you can train yourself to find that peak level of performance that comes from within and improves your experience of life and the experience of those with whom you engage.

If you choose to train yourself, you may join the ranks of those who claim an exponentially improved existence, unavailable before they attained and maintained their flow state. ***Because every person's perspective is different, every path to flow is unique.***

Those who envisioned and attained the state found it invaluable to have a mentor who understood the several paths that can bring you to flow. Eastern and Western practices each have missing components that, when combined with each other and with other tools and frameworks, can be overcome.

Choose the path that will lead to your future.
Your future self awaits.

final words

History is a story being told by mankind. Together we are telling the story of now. Lead the world around you. Make it a place you are proud to live in and share with generations to come.

In this world, I have come to learn things fully but then hold them lightly. Life can change our viewpoints. Suffering comes when we hold on too tightly to what we think we know. Separating ourselves into artificial factions can be destructive to creation. It limits our resources, our service, and our power. We all know limits and labels are falsely created. They instantly go away when a plane is going down or when the world rises together against a perceived threat!

This book series is a song in my heart which is being sung to the deepest part of you. Maybe my dream will turn into a reality where we all become *fully empowered, conscious leaders creating a new and beautiful world.*

Are you ready to create a better world around you?

You are not alone.

This ends the Creating a Leader trilogy. It is time to put in place what will work for you. Our planet and your environment need the best you can offer right now. I will continue to work hard to offer solutions to become the best generation our planet has seen.
+10 Leaders will change this world for the better.
An adaptable species – we humans are!

Have fun creating...

...and let me know if I can help.

Made in the USA
Columbia, SC
08 August 2018